WARTIME IN WHITSTABLE

Remembered

WARTIME IN WHITSTABLE
Remembered

JESSIE VINE

EDITED AND COMPILED BY PAUL CRAMPTON

The History Press

First published 2012

The History Press
The Mill, Brimscombe Port
Stroud, Gloucestershire, GL5 2QG
www.thehistorypress.co.uk

British Library Cataloguing in Publication Data.
A catalogue record for this book is available from the British Library.

ISBN 978 0 7524 6124 3

Typesetting and origination by The History Press
Printed in Great Britain
Manufacturing managed by Jellyfish Print Solutions Ltd

CONTENTS

INTRODUCTION

This book is the second volume of my late maternal grandmother's memoirs. The first volume *Dover Remembered*, published by Meresborough Books in 1984, came out in her lifetime, and she therefore had complete control over every aspect of the project. (Although this book is out of print, second hand copies seem to crop up regularly in bookshops and on Internet sites). *Wartime in Whitstable Remembered* or, as it was originally to have been called, '*A Navy Wife's War Remembered*', was begun by her in the late 1980s, and intended to be a logical follow-up. Sadly, my late grandfather's poor health meant that the project had to be cancelled, and although she completed a typed manuscript, the book was taken no further. My grandfather, Tom Vine, did have a small involvement in this second book, completing three drawings for it, but his contribution was nothing like that to be found in the Dover volume. My beloved Grandad passed away in July 1991, at the age of eighty-four, and the Whitstable project was put in a drawer and forgotten.

As family archivist, I later inherited all of my grandmother's photographs and manuscripts (there are at least two other unpublished, illustrated books of poetry) and the Whitstable project was among them. With the current interest in all matters concerning the Second World War, I thought it timely to pursue the publication of this forgotten second volume, and The History Press were immediately keen to take it on board, hence the book you now hold in your hands. What clinched the deal though, was the vast archive of family, and other unique photographs that I would be able to liberally spread throughout the text.

Dover Remembered covered Jessie's childhood, in her hometown, from her birth in 1907 until roughly 1920, and the aftermath of the First World War. *Wartime in Whitstable Remembered* picks up the story of her life again in 1939. Therefore, I thought it useful, and also of interest, to include the key events in the life of Jessie Vine (née Tomlin) as part of this book's introduction.

The Tomlin family moved from no. 33 Trevanion Street, to no. 12 Effingham Crescent, at sometime during the 1920s. This was effectively a move across town, and also a deliberate relocation to a 'better' area of Dover. Jessie's first job was as a window sign-writer for Woolworth's in Dover. She prospered in this endeavour and was given advancement within the organisation, which meant that she had to travel all over East Kent to other branches, including Canterbury.

Throughout this period, Jessie continued to date her childhood sweetheart, Tom, who had by now signed up for a twenty-five-year stint in the Royal Navy. Being painfully shy, he never actually called for her at no. 12, but would wait at the end of the street, until she noticed him.

My grandfather's first significant ship posting was aboard HMS *Cumberland*, and this took him away from Jessie for months, even years at a time.

During Tom's absence, my grandmother sought alternative employment, and became a professional companion to a Mrs Du Pre, which meant her moving out of the area for the duration. The house she stayed at, when not on tour with her mistress, was Wilton Park, Beaconsfield in Buckinghamshire, which was usually referred to as the 'White House'. This three-storey Palladian mansion had been built in 1779 by Josias Du Pre and had remained in the same family ever since. Jessie had a room on an upper storey at the front of the house, overlooking the extensive landscaped gardens.

Later on, in 1939, Wilton Park would be leased to the War Office and, by 1942, had become a prisoner-of-war camp for high-ranking enemy officers, such as Rudolf Hess. So who knows, the former Vice-Chancellor of Nazi Germany may have stayed in the same room as my grandmother once had. Sadly, the 'White House' was demolished in 1968, to be replaced by what has been described as 'an ugly fifteen-storey accommodation block'.

My grandmother's new career as a lady's companion wouldn't last for long, however; love was calling in the form of a young, muscular Naval rating. Tom and Jessie finally married on 11 November 1932 and they honeymooned locally. For the first few months of their marriage, the couple lived at the Tomlin family home in Effingham Crescent. Before long, Jessie again sought new employment, and this time, decided to stand on her own two feet. Having inherited many, if not all, of her father's tailoring skills (from all those many hours of watching him at work atop his bench), she decided to strike out on her own and begin a one-woman dressmaking business. Her business card read as follows, 'Let Jessie Tomlin make your frocks, and ensure quick service, modern styles and reasonable charges.'

My grandparents subsequently found a flat in Russell Street, Dover, but a move to Rochester, in order to be nearer the dockyard at Chatham was also in the offing. This would enable my grandfather to better continue participating in the RN Barracks Field Gun Crew, which competed at Olympia every year. (Later on, as Petty Officer, or Chief Petty Officer, my grandfather would go on to train that same competitive crew.) Another tour of duty aboard HMS *Cumberland* subsequently beckoned, but by the time Tom came home again in early 1935, it was to a rented house in City Way, Rochester.

This was a house they shared with Tom's sister Ivy, her husband Sid Hookham (another Naval man) and their young son Bob. My mother, Joy, was born in October 1935, at the RN Hospital in Gillingham. There were terrible complications during the birth, and my grandmother very nearly died. As a result, she had to spend months in hospital afterwards and, although she mostly recovered, was not able to have any further children. In the meantime, my mother was raised by Connie Tomlin, who was the wife of Jessie's brother, Charlie. These temporary foster parents then lived in Howard Avenue, which backed on to the house in City Way. Incidentally, Joy was named after one of Colonel and Mrs Du Pre's three daughters.

A significant event in Tom's life was being given the honour of hauling the gun carriage that carried the coffin of George V at his state funeral. He was one of many such Naval ratings to have taken part, but his position was in the front row, as left-marker, because of his height and strength. The funeral took place on 28 January 1936, and the procession saw the coffin of the late king, atop a gun carriage, being taken from lying-in-state at Westminster Hall, to the funeral service at St George's Chapel, Windsor.

Even though my grandfather had become a Petty Officer by this time, for the funeral procession, he had to assume the traditional 'square-rig' of a Naval rating. The men in front of the gun carriage had to maintain the strain and the direction of the assemblage, while those behind it acted as brake-men, preventing the carriage from running away, or the connecting ropes from slacking in the middle.

After the event, my grandfather was awarded the Royal Victorian Medal (silver) by the future Edward VIII. He was also given a commemorative photograph album, to acknowledge his service on that day, which contained a personal handwritten message from Queen Mary herself. These treasured items are still in my possession today.

Also, in 1936, Sid Hookham was posted to Malta, and took his family with him. At around the same time, Tom, Jessie and their tiny daughter Joy moved to a semi-detached bungalow at no. 9 Howard Avenue, near to where a number of relatives already resided.

By 1938 Tom was touring the world in the converted training ship HMS *Vindictive*, which allowed him to regularly 'pop in' on his sister's family in Malta. Meanwhile, back in Howard Avenue, my grandmother had her hands full with my high-spirited mother, as she became an active toddler.

Paul Crampton, 2012

1

HAPPY DAYS

I raised the clothes prop as high as it would go, until the galvanised line was stretched as taut as possible, and the newly washed clothes were swinging in the breeze of that bright July morning. I had awakened very early indeed, about four o'clock, and could not rest content any longer because of the rising tide of excitement and anticipation of the coming day. It was to be a very special day.

While I scrubbed more garments in the hot suds in the kitchen sink, I was unconsciously singing softly to myself,

> Blow him again to me
> While my little one, while my pretty one
> Sleeps . . .
> Sleep and rest, sleep and rest
> Father will come to thee soon
> Father will come to his babe in the nest
> Silver sails from out of the west.
> Blow him again to me,
> While my little one, while my pretty one
> Sleeps . . .

But there were no silver sails around him wherever he was, but funnels, superstructure, guns and the grim paraphernalia of warfare. I paused in my work and continued to sing, tapping out the rhythm on the galvanised washboard that was pressed to my waterproof apron, and I drifted away for a few moments in daydreams. 'While my little one sleeps' – but Joy wouldn't wake for another hour or so. I peeped in at her, soundly sleeping, clutching her doll, all so peaceful. She would also be having an exciting day.

Having finished all my laundry work, and feeling satisfied that it would soon be dry and ready for ironing, I knew that I had ample time to get everything around the home ship-shape by midday. I liked it all to be bright and cheerful with flowers for his homecoming, with slippers at the ready, pipe rack in evidence, and civvy clothes laid out on the bed.

Tom would be so pleased to abandon his uniform and pretend that he was a landlubber for a while, do a bit of gardening, and a few odd jobs around the bungalow that had been awaiting his attention. A sailor's wife is usually a very versatile person, having learnt by virtue of necessity to find out how to do jobs for herself, but there are always a few things that needed a man's touch.

HMS *Vindictive*, the training ship, berthed at Malta, during the mid-1930s.

I heard a few scuffling noises coming from the bedroom, and peeping in, there she was, my little girl, sitting up sleepily rubbing her eyes, her bonny curls all awry like a cloud of spun silk.

'Do you remember what's going to happen today?' I asked. With a squeal of delight, and a sudden brightening of expression, she said, 'Yes, Daddy's coming home today. I wonder what he'll bring this time?'

Children have a wonderful memory for things like that, and Joy knew that her Daddy would never forget to bring her presents. Tom was on a three-month cruise in the Mediterranean, on HMS *Vindictive*, with the young cadet officers-in-training straight from Dartmouth Naval College. He was, at that time, a Petty Officer Gunnery Instructor. The ship was due in at Chatham Dockyard for summer leave.

My four-year-old and I had breakfast and were just about to commence the usual chores, when two men arrived.

'Are you ready for your Anderson shelter, ma' am?' One of them called.

'Oh, yes please. Do you want to start now?'

And they did – working quickly and efficiently, digging a large hole in our little patch of garden. The Anderson was a shell of corrugated steel, 6ft long and was supposed to be buried 4ft deep in the earth. The width, just over 4ft, was enough to allow sleeping arrangements to be made. We found out later, that water seeped in freely, and if folk had to spend long hours inside, then it would have become a health hazard. However, as a protection from bombs, it would have served its purpose, unless there was a direct hit.

I was concerned for my washing just then, for the upheaval of the dry soil was creating dust clouds all around the centre of activity. We had all experienced a very dry spell of weather

Young Joy helps the men to install the Anderson shelter in the back garden of no. 9 Howard Avenue, Rochester. The rear elevations of houses in City Way can be seen in the background.

and our few pansies were struggling for existence. Only the weeds seemed lively, but then they always do.

Joy's concern was lest the men should spoil her newly made sand pit, but the men assured her that it would be safe, so she wanted to help them dig. In fact, it soon became clear that she was torn between two desires: one, to watch the men's activities, and the other, to wait at the gate for her Daddy's arrival. Therefore, her time was spent alternating between both interests, her chubby little legs carrying her with remarkable speed from one place to the other so as not to miss anything.

Glancing at the clock inside, I saw that the morning was still young. Yes – all was tidy, I thought to myself, and doesn't the place look different with this additional furniture. I gazed lovingly at the new three-piece suite with pride. It had only been delivered the previous day, and I had shuffled it round and about, placing and replacing until I was satisfied. On each of Tom's three-month cruises, I had aimed to save up to buy a new item that would be a surprise for him on his arrival home.

It wasn't easy to save, but I had been brought up to watch the pennies and by dint of much perseverance, I had managed it, and here it was! No hire purchase for me – it had all been paid for. And how very nice it looked, with its lovely blend of fawns and greenery, and it also looked so inviting. Oh yes, Tom would like it!

I set to work preparing a favourite dinner and soon the succulent aroma was making the workmen in the garden sniff the air longingly, so I took them out a pot of tea, and looked at their progress. It was amazing how rapidly they had worked.

Jessie tries out the newly installed Anderson shelter, during the last months of peace in 1939.

'We've done a good many of these up to now,' said the older man, as he paused for a while. 'Perhaps they won't be needed after all. But there you are; just in case. Neville Chamberlain says it's going to be alright now, so please God, war won't come!'

'Amen to that,' I replied, 'there are so many servicemen's families around these parts and they are all anxious, but then, I suppose it's the same all over the country. Everyone will be affected.'

'Yes, that's right,' the older man replied, 'but let's give you some advice about this 'ere shelter.' He gestured towards the newly erected structure. 'First, you should set about getting yourself some duckboards, for on this slope, you'll certainly get waterlogged, and you may want to put some bedding in there. And it's a good idea to get some quick-growing plants growing on the top; after all, it's covered with soil!'

When the men had finally left, I looked at the monstrosity that now filled up most of the garden space, and it brought the whole realisation home to me: of changes looming on the horizon; of how the whole nation had been anxiously watching events of the previous few months. Earlier in the year before, Austria had been annexed by Germany, and during this year of 1939, nerves were being stretched taut.

In retrospect, the people criticised the agreement made between Chamberlain, Daladier, Mussolini and Hitler on 29 September 1938. It all seemed to have been a useless venture, and had proved nothing at all, except that Hitler was a sham and Neville Chamberlain had been conned. Of course, he had meant well, but was too trusting, and Hitler was no gentleman. As Caesar had said of Cassius, 'such men are dangerous'. The appeasement policy had also prompted some scathing remarks from the Rt Hon Winston Churchill.

Mr Chamberlain had said, waving the paper on which Hitler had placed his signature, 'all this will be over in three months,' and he went on to use these words, 'this is the second time that there has come back from Germany to Downing Street, peace with honour. I believe it is peace in our time.' The cheerful gesturing of the famous umbrella became a joke. Events in Europe continued to upset both people and statesmen alike, and everyone began to wonder what would happen next.

Conscription had started in the spring of 1939, and evacuation schemes had been planned. Thousands of civilian respirators had already been manufactured and widely distributed at the time of the Munich Crisis. The very thought of being gassed, like the poor wretched Tommies in the trenches of the First World War absolutely horrified us, especially when we were given more details. We were told that poison gas could smell like pear drops, or musty hay, or even geraniums,

The Navy recruitment photo that featured Tom, and of which Jessie was so proud!

Tom arrives home from Chatham Dockyard following his 1939 cruise aboard HMS *Vindictive*.

For now though, I had to clear my mind of these unsettling thoughts on this special day – I had to check on the liver and bacon casserole that was simmering in the oven, and then put the sugar sprinkling on the apple pie. Tradition demanded that there would always be an apple pie made when a sailor came home from the sea. In fact, the standing joke was that apple pie would be the second thing he asked for.

I just couldn't contain myself to stay indoors any longer. And so, I quickly laid the table and, taking a final look around, together with a satisfying pat of the cushions, went out to the front gate to join Joy. We waited, stooping occasionally to pull up a stray weed here and there, all the time keeping a keen lookout up to the end of the road, where his taxi would soon be appearing. Oh dear, how time drags when one is waiting!

A blackbird in the tree next door eyed me quizzically; he was trying to tell me that I had forgotten his usual tit-bits. I thought back to other homecomings, and that familiar aroma that always enveloped Tom when he came straight from shipboard: a curious mixture of carbolic soap and strong tobacco. Sailors are among the cleanest people in the world – woe betide any who defaulted, but they seldom ever did; their messmates would quickly see to that.

A passing neighbour asked if I was expecting my husband home, and told me she was on her way to collect her gas mask.

'I hate the idea of these respirators,' she said. 'Do you know that they even have them for young babies? But perhaps we'll never need them anyway.'

I hoped that she would not stay there chatting when Tom arrived. I kept on looking to the end of the road, and was so glad when she eventually moved away. 'Goodbye Mrs D!'

Most of the people near about, being Navy folk, took a keen interest in Tom, because his picture had been seen all over the British Isles and also the Empire, when the Admiralty had photographed him for a recruiting poster about eighteen months earlier. In fact, it was on exactly the same day that the Crystal Palace in London had burned down. Tom had to dress in the rig of a Chief Engine-room Artificer for the occasion and, as he was actually a gunnery man, all the badges on his own uniform had to be replaced by those of an ERA I had the job of doing that! He went to London for the photographic session, for which he was posed at the salute. They also attempted to sink his identity to some extent, by making his otherwise blond hair appear as dark. Afterwards, I had to replace the original badges. Imagine my surprise and dismay then, when I had to go through the same performance all over again in the following week, when the Admiralty decided they wanted to do a repeat session.

 I was very proud of that recruiting poster, especially when I saw it in full length on the screen at the local cinema. On the few occasions that Tom had been home from leave, and had accompanied me to the pictures, I found myself gesturing towards him when the recruiting poster appeared, as if to say, 'look, here he is in the flesh!' In turn, poor Tom, ever the self-effacing and shy man that he was, would sink ever further into his seat, desperate for the moment to pass.

My chatty neighbour waved her hand encouragingly when she moved to the corner of the road, and then my heart leapt – such a sight was nearing the gate. It was difficult to make out at first, but then I could gradually see what it was. There were several basketwork chairs lashed to the top of a taxi, piled high and all in a heap, and it took quite a while to get them all down. The cheery-looking driver had probably seen it all before, while bringing sailors home from foreign parts, and no longer registered any surprise at all the things he would be expected to carry.

It wasn't exactly the greeting that I had anticipated, for most of the neighbours were peeping out to see what all the commotion was about, and Joy was dancing round with delight at seeing three chairs of different sizes, which she declared were, 'one for Daddy Bear, one for Mummy Bear and one for Baby Bear.'

Once they'd been unloaded, it didn't take very long to get those bulky pieces of furniture into the bungalow, and then for us to have our hugs and kisses away from other people's eyes.

We quickly fell into a steady routine for three people instead of two, and spent some delightful days of summer, enjoying happy country walks among the birds, trees and flowers. Nature seemed at its very best, with simple delights and surprises to be found everywhere. We took picnics and spent many hours just lazing the time away, while Tom would sketch everything in sight. This was his favourite hobby, especially when we came across old buildings. What a wonderful change from the sea: that unpredictable element that can be so beautiful and then so fiercely cruel.

Tom, Joy and I were happy – very happy, and I desperately tried to forget that war-fever was already spoiling so many other people's way of life. But I wasn't letting it spoil ours for the brief time that we had together, so I hid our gas masks in a cupboard and decided not to tell my husband that I had been to the council offices to find out what sort of war work could be done by a woman with a small child – if war should come. Yes, I had to forget all of that for a while and pretend that the rumblings and rumours of war had never happened. As things turned out, Tom would be on the ship in Chatham Dockyard for a few weeks, until the next cruise started, so there would be weekend leave to look forward to and, in all probability, most nights at home for that period, so why worry about the possible war just yet?

During this period, Tom also had some studying to do, and so brought various papers home with him on the theory of gunnery. He'd always been besotted with sports and had taken no real interest in learning until, having acquired a wife and child, he realised the necessity of hard work for advancement in his chosen career. So, for now, he forgot all about water polo, putting the shot, tug-of-war and boat-pulling. He had been champion of the China Fleet for putting the shot, when he served on HMS *Cumberland*, and had also taken many parts in the Field Gun Crews at Olympia until, eventually, he actually trained the Chatham crew. Now, however, there was work to do, so we spread the papers on the table, during those long summer evenings, and tackled logarithms and trigonometry together. I soon learned by heart the drill sequence of a 15-inch gun turret, and could almost have drilled a gun crew myself.

A joke among gunnery instructors was that, if a wife should be asked to perform at a party, she would say, 'I can't sing, I can't dance, but being a gunnery man's wife, I'll give you a few movements of the rifle on the march.'

Finally, the summer days began to shorten, and the wild rose bushes, once a profusion of simple white flowers, were now beginning to show their red berries. All around us, bountiful nature was providing plenty of treasure in the hedgerows for the wild animals and birds to store for the coming winter. There was no looking too far forward for us though. We lived for each day as it came, happy as always, and Joy was so delighted that her Daddy was home again with us virtually all the time. She also hoped that he would not have to go away again, but he did.

When he did finally go to war, Tom would be away for over two years.

2

THE EXODUS

Life seemed so dull and empty with we two on our own again, and the war rumbles were getting louder every day, striking fear and apprehension into the hearts of many wives and mothers. And then, Hitler invaded Poland on 1 September and feelings ran high. The stories that began filtering through filled us with sorrow for that beleaguered country.

We all criss-crossed our windows with paper strips and made hasty blackout curtains. Inevitably, as the demand for this commodity increased, the supplies ran out and the price increased also. Many householders had to improvise, using blankets, and rugs, or any old thing that came to hand, until a better job could be done. Newly appointed air raid wardens kept a keen watch for chinks of light that might show and be a guide for the enemy. Indeed, by this time, we all felt that we certainly had an enemy. All sorts of things began to happen with feverish haste, and although we tried to think, or hope, that it was all a false alarm, we seemed to know that war was now inevitable.

The evacuation scheme for school children began to take shape in earnest and instructions were sent out to all schools. The local schools and councils in Rochester and Chatham willingly co-operated on the details of the plan's implementation, as there was a definite sense of urgency by this time.

I went again to the council offices and was told that I could be very useful, so I promptly went to see the headmistress of one of the Rochester schools. On my way there, I felt rather alarmed to see that sand bags were being stacked against important buildings, and trenches were being dug in the parks and leisure grounds.

Having arrived at my destination, I was very impressed by the lady at the school. She was a typical headmistress: strong in character, a large lady with a large heart, I thought. And so it proved to be, for she was to become a source of inspiration for us all.

'You are just what we need,' she said, 'I'm so short of teachers and helpers.'

After a short conversation, she decided that my little one could be entered on the registers as a pupil, although she was only four years old. That way, Joy could be called an evacuee and join the party with me. So, I was to act as teacher-cum-helper and be able to keep my child under my wing as well. [Editor's note: Although my grandmother does not mention the name of the specific school, I believe that it was St Peter's Infant, or Primary, School, in Holcombe Road, Rochester.]

My sister-in-law, Ivy Hookham, also a sailor's wife with one small son, Bob, joined the group at the same time. Ivy and I were also the greatest of friends, and so we both felt a sense of some relief that our new situation would at least mean that we'd be near to each other.

Our respective husbands would also take great comfort from that. So we were not entirely among strangers, although we had no idea where we might be sent.

Friday 1 September: It was with much heart-searching that I packed a suitcase for myself and a smaller one for Joy, took a last look around my little home at all those familiar things, and then turned the key in the lock with a sad feeling of loss. The last glimpse that I had as I left the garden, was the bright and beautiful array of nasturtiums on the top of the Anderson shelter. It seemed like a ray of hope – there was still some beauty in the world after all. On the way to the school grounds, I posted a letter to Tom c/o 'somewhere at sea', I knew not where. When would I see him again? What would happen to all of us now?

Joy was very puzzled at all the strange happenings, but thrilled to be among lots of other children. I had purchased a blue blazer and beret for her, so that she would look more like a little schoolgirl than a child scarcely more than a toddler. She looked so sweet, with her bright curls bobbing up and down from under the beret, which she didn't like one little bit, and it kept finding its way into her pocket.

We assembled in the school playground, each child labelled according to plan, with a boxed gasmask slung around each little neck. Every child carried a container of some sort: carrier bags, small Woolworth's cardboard suitcases, and a good many of them hugged nothing more than a brown paper parcel tied up with string. They had all been given instructions to take home to parents, specifying all the necessities to be packed for the evacuation, but for how long? Nobody knew the answer to that question. Some mothers had made poor efforts to fulfil the requirements, while others had done far more than was manageable, burdening the children with cases far too large to carry comfortably. I was surprised to see so many Wellington boots being worn on this warm autumn day, until one boy told me that it was, 'much easier to wear 'em than to carry 'em!' That made sense!

Joy thought that this was all great fun as we marched to Rochester railway station, and there was a good deal of excitement at the sight of all those 'puffer trains'. Joy had already found a little companion, and they were holding hands like bosom pals. Many mothers trailed along with us, some with babies, fearful of letting their beloved offspring go away to unknown homes for an indefinite period. Moist handkerchiefs concealed the sadness, for the children would be even more unsettled and upset if they saw mothers in tears. Everyone knew that they had to be brave – after all, there might be a war.

'Were they downhearted?' A reproduction of the newspaper picture showing some Rochester children at the railway station on Friday 1 September 1939, just prior to boarding their evacuation train. Jessie has marked herself, Joy and cousin Bob.

I was in the fortunate position of having Ivy – not only a much-loved sister-in-law, but also a close friend – travelling with me in the same outfit. We shared the same anxieties and misgivings as to the whereabouts of our husbands, so we were able to console each other as we threw ourselves into the job in hand. Indeed, there was much to be done and plenty to fill our minds given the present situation. Each of us was responsible for an individual group of these oddly assorted children, of varying ages.

To the youngsters, the journey was a thrill. All were greatly exhilarated at the thoughts of the seaside, but still no-one knew exactly where we would end up. I remembered many picturesque coves along the Thanet coast, but I would have preferred a quiet place in the country away from the sea, under present conditions. However, the powers-that-be knew best and so we set off for our, as-yet, unknown Kentish seaside resort.

As the train pulled out of the station, in an eastwards direction, it was almost impossible to control the groups. Some started to be tearful at the thought of leaving parents behind, while others wet themselves with excitement. Some even began to feel sick. Oh dear, there were no corridors on this particular train. In any case, we adults did our best to cheer them all up, by telling of the great fun that we would have building sandcastles and paddling.

On our 'mystery journey', we passed many grimy backyards and sooty chimney pots, and the windows of every house were made shabbier still by the assorted arrangements of brown paper stuck to them. However, we soon reached the beautiful fields of the Kentish countryside, and could marvel at the huge drifts of scarlet poppies and cheerful marguerites. Everything seemed so bright and glorious with the sun shining on the long grasses, so that the gentle breeze made it look like waves in the sea. Inevitably, I thought of Tom once more.

Further eastwards still, and the children soon scrambled to see the rolling orchards with trees laden with ripe apples, and the regimented hop gardens, all ready for the harvesting.

> From Kent's productive acres,
> come very special crops.
> Luscious, juicy apples
> and sweetly smelling hops.
> A merry band of pickers,
> need weather warm and fine,
> then busily, with speedy skill,
> scratch hops from off the vine.
> They're gathered in the oast house,
> Kept drying for the beers,
> And then in Kentish taverns,
> A rousing cry of CHEERS.

Some of the children had already started to unfasten little parcels of food, which fond parents had earlier stuffed into their pockets. At the same time, I prompted them to sing and very appropriately the choice was 'All Things Bright and Beautiful', which happened to be Tom's favourite hymn. I couldn't help thinking that it was so awful that mankind could not be content with all of God's wonderful gifts, and that the lust for power of a few, should make such an upheaval in the lives of so many. But this was not the time to muse on the behaviour of warlords; we had children to look after, and the excitement was beginning to get too much.

'How can we clean this compartment?'

'Please Miss, Billy's been sick!'

'Mary, have you got clean knickers in your case?'

'Johnny, have you got a handkerchief? Then use it.'

'Don't worry, it won't be long now.'

We were glad to be finally approaching Canterbury, for that comparatively short journey had been chaotic. But now we could see the River Stour to our right and, better still, we were offered our first sight of Canterbury Cathedral, which dominated the distant horizon. Our journey's end was nearing; at least as far as rail travel was concerned. The train passed through the suburb of Wincheap, with its neat rows of red-brick houses, and then as it began to slow down, the beautiful cathedral came into view once more, this time on our left side, and also much closer than before. The train soon came to rest on the Down platform of Canterbury East. [Editor's note: My mother Joy recalls a slightly different journey, and remembers that the train went directly from Rochester to Whitstable station. Indeed, there would be no need for it to first go to Canterbury (East) and then for the passengers to have an unnecessary bus ride across country to the coast. In her memoirs, my grandmother may indeed having been recalling the end of a train journey at a different time, but I have left her original words intact, as none of us can be 100 per cent sure which version is the correct one.]

The busy scene of a typical evacuation train departure. This particular image was taken at Canterbury East station.

3

BILLETING

Lining up the groups outside the station, we waited while our indomitable leader fussed around like a mother hen, checking all her little charges, and giving words of comfort and encouragement to the tearful ones. Soon, two coaches came along and we all climbed aboard. We hadn't travelled many miles before someone shouted that they could see the sea on the distant horizon. Then squeals of delight filled the coach and tears were wiped away as the contentment spread with the anticipation of pleasures to come: sand, sea and sunshine. What a lovely thought! Even at this stage, we were not quite certain of our destination, but one place would be as good as another along that coast, we all decided; just so long as it was considered to be safe in these troubled times.

Swalecliffe Road, Tankerton, in the late 1930s, and the sort of street scene that made an immediate impression on Jessie.

We were soon travelling along tree-lined roads, and I was struck with the pristine cleanliness that prevailed. We also saw well-kept gardens, laid out with flowering shrubs and colourful beds of varied flowers. And all the houses looked so opulent. I thought of the squalid streets that we had left behind in the Medway towns, many of which were so out-dated as to be virtual slums – only in the outskirts had the scene been changing with some groups of modern houses appearing here and there. However, the place that we were now entering was all that one could desire – no rough-looking dwellings that I could see, no grimy backyards and no shabby people. It was all as pretty as a picture. The question was: what would these genteel-looking people make of us?

There was a general consensus reached that we were about to reach the end of the journey, and so it proved to be. In no time at all, we were scrambling from the coach, and the children were asked to assemble in orderly groups. That done, they anxiously waited to see what would happen next. By this time, there were many onlookers watching our roll call, as we checked all the personnel labels, pulled skirts into place and wiped a few sticky faces.

At last, we were told that we had arrived in Whitstable, and that we would be billeted right here, in this particularly delightful suburb of the old fishing and cockling town. The well-appointed suburb itself was called Tankerton.

Since Roman times, Whitstable has been famous for its oysters, believed by the gourmet, and claimed by some avid consumers, to be aphrodisiac. At the turn of the century, the town had a fleet of oyster smacks and harvested 50 million oysters a year. In the old town, many of the local folk were associated with the harbour and its various activities. However, the sleepy suburb to which we had been assigned appeared to be populated with elderly and retired people.

Our particular evacuee gathering went into the grounds of a very large school where ladies and officials were standing in groups ready to sort out who was going where, and with whom. The local people then distributed carrier bags containing various groceries, which had been

A typical scene at the busy Whitstable Harbour, with both ships and railway wagons visible.

Having been selected for billeting by local residents, Ivy Hookham's group departs from St Mary's School, and begins to head up Northwood Road, Tankerton.

contributed by the authorities. [Editor's note: My grandmother does not mention the name of the school, but I have been told that it was St Alphege's School, in Oxford Street, Whitstable. The other coach – containing the group led by Ivy Hookham – dropped off at a different location, being St Mary's Roman Catholic School, in Northwood Road. Incidentally, the coaches were driven by the Bottle brothers, who came from Dover and actually knew my grandfather Tom from the pre-war years.]

I began to wonder if these Medway children would fit in with this community, and doubts gradually filled my mind. Lucky, as time would prove, my worries were unfounded, and the children fitted in very well.

Those among the prospective carers of these little evacuees of war, who clearly had experience with children, were quick to make up their minds and were swiftly moving away with their new charges in tow: strange little lodgers for 10s per week, per child. On the other hand, some of the grander ladies took much longer to choose their temporary boarders, and spent a lot of time checking on the condition of each one, examining hair, clothes and hands. Fortunately, human nature is at its very best when there's trouble about – compassion prevailed and the ranks of evacuees began to thin out.

4

THE MISTAKE

Joy did not leave my side, but clung to my skirts as I moved here and there, writing down names and addresses so that mothers could be notified. However, for a few moments I lost sight of her, but knowing that the gate of the school compound was closed, I was not unduly worried. However, a hurried glance around showed me what had taken her interest. She had seen a little dog – she'd always loved animals. There was a time when she was at a party along the street, and when she was brought home, she had a puppy under her arm. On this occasion, I found her in the company of an elderly lady, who was holding a tiny rat-like creature to her bosom, wrapped in a scarlet blanket. It lay, blinking its watery eyes, while Joy was admiring the odd little thing. We soon learned that it was a Chihuahua, a breed from Mexico, very small and smooth-haired, obviously the pride and delight of its mistress. For the moment though, this lady was sizing up the small child as a prospective lodger.

I saw her raise the little dress to examine the state of Joy's underwear. However, she had no need to remove the beret for hair examination, for the offending article had, once again, been stuffed into her blazer pocket. The elderly lady lifted the golden curls and, as I approached, she said, 'I'll take this one!'

I stood for a moment, lost for words. Of course, Joy had to be placed somewhere, but not without me.

'If you have her, you'll have me too. I'm her mother,' I said with a smile, meanwhile taking stock of her, just as thoroughly as she was taking stock of me.

The old woman told me her name and declared that she had only anticipated having one child, but with a further glance at the diminishing ranks, she said, 'Well, in that case, I'll take you both in.'

She was a wiry bird-like woman, with an aquiline nose, and keen, intelligent eyes. One had the impression that nothing escaped her eagle-like gaze. For my part, I must have looked far from my best, after the trauma of the last two-and-a-half hours. Hot and perspiring freely, on this bright late summer's day, I was aware of a tear in my stocking caused by a small boy's feet, stuck out from the seat in the railway carriage. My suede shoes were badly scuffed, having been stood on many times in the evacuation train – and I'd also lost my lace gloves.

By contrast, she was so immaculate, which made me feel somewhat inferior. Her well-cut tweed costume was in the very best taste – the epitome of good tailoring. The set of the shoulders and the perfect revers told me so. My father had been a tailor back in Dover, and so I knew about these things. I also took in the quality of her brogues and expensive-looking jewellery.

Priest and Sow Corner, between Tankerton and Swalecliffe, in the period immediately before the Second World War. Note the tearoom on the corner.

The same Priest and Sow tearoom, after anti-invasion defences had been put in place. On Tankerton seafront, defences were installed all the way along the top of the Slopes, as well as in interrupted lengths along the beach itself. *(Photograph courtesy of Messenger Group Newspapers)*

It occurred to me that it was only just September, and very warm weather for the time of year, yet she was wearing such heavy clothing, and Joy and I were both hot and sticky in the heat. Her slight frame seemed barely covered with flesh, so I supposed that she needed thicker clothing than the rest of us. However, her face had a ruddy glow, which made me think that she might be a health food fanatic. This proved to be the case, as I learned to my cost during the next eighteen hours.

Later, as I got to know the lady better, I had great admiration for her brave effort to do her bit for the evacuee cause, thereby disrupting her peaceful way of life where she had only her little dogs to care for. The very idea of sharing her home with anyone else must have been abhorrent, but no-one could say that she did not come forward when duty called. [Editor's note: Because of the less-than-ideal circumstances my family were soon to find themselves in, Jessie was reluctant to name the lady in question, always fearful of causing offence, even years afterwards. However, I don't think there can be any harm, or embarrassment, caused now by saying that the woman was a Miss Ship, from Graystone Road, Tankerton. She must have been a relative newcomer to the area, as she does not appear in mid-1930s street directories.]

We walked along several roads and again I was impressed with the style and quality of Tankerton's houses and bungalows. We soon came to her house and my first thought was that it looked like a little palace. The garden was in impeccable order, with the plants set in regimented rows and not a weed in sight. An ornamental statue stood sentinel over all. The door was oaken with the finest brass knocker that I had ever seen, and when she opened the door and ushered us inside, it was all I could do not to gasp. However, I also realised that I'd be afraid to move, in case I knocked anything out of place, and as for Joy – she'd have to be good, very good. There'd be no charging up and down the stairs; no swinging on door handles.

A chorus of yapping brought me down to earth, and I realised that the red-blanketed pet that Joy had so admired was not the only one. There were two more of these little creatures, blinking up at us, too tired to get out of their luxurious beds, but very much inclined to show displeasure at the presence of intruders. I was informed by my new landlady that they were the mother and aunt of the little one she'd been carrying.

First, we had to find our slippers, for the carpet was a light colour and looked as if it had never been trodden on. I had always been interested in antiques, and here was a feast for the eyes, and I longed to take a closer look at these treasures, but for the moment there were more mundane things to think about. Next, our hostess took us upstairs and it was immediately obvious that she had, as already stated, planned for only one child. However, she suggested that a folding bed in the loft could be brought down for my use, but being anxious not to give any trouble, I told her that a 3ft bed would be enough for the two of us – plenty of room for a mother who would want to hold her little one tightly in the night – fearful that fate might part them.

I had intended to write to my husband, to tell him of our new address, but there would be no mail collection the following day, it being a Sunday. Instead, tea was the next thing that happened, and a small table was duly laid with an exquisite lace embroidered cloth, upon which had been placed a plate with four wafer-like slices of bread and butter, and six biscuits from our gift carrier bags, which looked lost on that large plate.

There was a teapot of China tea for the lady, placed near the dogs' baskets, and another pot of Indian for us. Our hostess seated herself on a beautiful velvet chair and proceeded to feed the little animals with small pieces of biscuit.

Joy and I were glad of a drink, whatever it was, which we did not handle with the same air of refinement as the lady did – in fact, we were so parched that we simply gulped it down. The idea of food was not enticing though, as there was a large lump in my throat – my heart was too full. I kept thinking of Tom and the comfortable little home I'd left behind in Rochester. This cold, sterile and terribly posh place suddenly seemed so alien: no familiar things, no love, no Tom, no Anderson shelter. Would I have been wiser to have stayed there and chanced the outcome? Tom had said it was necessary to go, so here we were. But how could I ever be happy under these circumstances? Worrying by day, unsleeping by night, and imagining all sorts of things.

I put Joy to bed early, for the poor child was exhausted after the day's events, and I sat in the lounge with my new host. I then helped her hang her blackout curtains. Like a good many people, she had made hasty efforts to secure a complete covering, and used the first thing available. In this case, it was a handsome piece of heavy tweed. I felt its fine quality and conjectured what a beautiful coat I could have made from it. I loved needlework and was in the habit of making everything we wore. I had begrudged the purchase of that ready-made school blazer that I'd had to get in a hurry for Joy, as there wasn't time to make one. While hanging the heavy blackout curtains, I observed the enormous stitches (Tom would have called them homeward-bounders) and concluded that this lady was no seamstress.

Afterwards, I tried to read the newspaper, but blurred eyes, partly from the lack of sleep and also from emotion, made it almost impossible, but I was going through the motions to make the situation easier, for conversation was practically non-existent.

Finally, I suggested I go to bed, and I was told not to turn on any lights upstairs, as there were no blackouts completed for the upper rooms. It was half-light, so a quick wash in the bathroom was easy enough, and I made sure that it was left exactly as I had found it. Taking my towel back to the bedroom and placing it on the back of a chair, I partially undressed. I had a fearful feeling that I must not remove all my clothes – something might happen in the night. But what could happen? It was not war yet, and surely there would be a warning anyway.

However, I lay down beside my child and the tears flowed noiselessly. I didn't want to wake her from innocent sleep.

5

THE FIRST WARNING

The next morning dawned to a beautiful day. The leaves on the trees outside were already taking on a wonderful russet shade. A few leaves had even started to fall, and the light, late summer breeze was blowing them along the road. I had been up since five o'clock, standing at the window looking at the unfamiliar world outside – taking stock of my new surroundings.

A busy milkman hurried down the street placing bottles on the well-kept doorsteps, taking care to close the gates, I noticed. He probably knew all his customers, and would be very careful not to offend them by leaving gates open. A ginger cat followed him all the way hoping for some early refreshment, but the cardboard tops were all firmly on the bottles. I also saw the paperboy putting fat bundles of newspapers into the letterboxes, and I hoped one was coming to this house. I desperately wanted to know what was happening in the world outside, but it turned out that no papers were delivered to this particular house on a Sunday!

At about 07.30, there were movements downstairs and I went to help with anything that needed to be done, but the Chihuahua's breakfast was the most important thing. Watching some lambs' liver frying in the pan, and then being mixed with chicken, certainly made my mouth water and I really felt hungry for breakfast. The dainty creatures sniffed at the gorgeous food disinterestedly and, after much persuasion, made a lazy effort to eat it,

'Come on, darlings, have your brekkie. Eat it up for Mummy.'

They did her the favour of eating a little, while Joy and I were upstairs getting dressed, and that appetising smell drifted to us. Soon, we went downstairs feeling much better than before, and opening the window to take a few breaths of fresh air, made me realise that the sea must be very close. It was only at the end of the road, I was told.

And now for breakfast, I thought; I'm ready for it. The table was laid with two spoons, two knives and two slices of dainty bread and butter, and on the stove I found a pan of porridge.

A voice from upstairs called out, 'Help yourselves to the porridge. Don't leave any; I don't eat breakfast!'

When we were seated, I looked at Joy's face.

'Is there any sugar, Mummy?' she asked.

There wasn't, so we ate it as it was, just as our host came into the room.

'That's right, it's the only way to eat porridge – with salt!' she said. And then I was certain that she was Scottish.

After the meal, we went out into the sunshine, having been told to be back by one o'clock for lunch. I made a beeline for our leader's lodgings in nearby Queens Road. We found her comfortably established in the cosy home of a plump homely lady with silver hair and a happy,

Having arrived in Tankerton, Jessie (left) and Ivy (right) gather some of the evacuated children together for a group photo. Joy is in the centre of the picture, and Bob is to her left.

round face that seemed to be always alight with her generous smile. I told our leader that I couldn't go on – that I'd rather go back to Rochester. I was sorry, but it wasn't the place for me – we just didn't fit in.

She soon made me feel that such action would be folly, and I realised that I must not be guilty of the sin of ingratitude. However, her quick brain soon had an answer to the problem. She knew of two ladies a few doors away, who were willing to have two evacuees and she felt sure that I would like them.

Our leader urged me to go back to the house I'd left and gave me a note to the effect that, owing to the large amount of correspondence, etc. to do, it was necessary for me to be nearer her – she would be obliged if Mrs Vine could move to enable us to get the work done. Apologies, etc, etc.

It wasn't possible to go back straight away as the children had to be rounded up from the neighbouring houses. They had been told to be at their gates by ten o'clock, so we took them to a nearby church hall and held an impromptu Sunday School, and listened to a few individual adventures. Most of the children were overawed by all that they had seen, and I must say, they all looked fresher than they had on the previous day. We only stayed together for about half an hour, and then we saw them back to their various billets.

On our way back to Graystone Road, we met a lady who, with great agitation, said that war had been declared. Britain had issued an ultimatum to the Germans that they should withdraw their troops from Poland, and by eleven o'clock there had been no reply, so consequently, Mr Chamberlain told the nation that he 'regretted that a state of war now existed between Great Britain and Germany.'

Joy and I proceeded to our lodging of one night, to present the note, and bring our things away. I had hoped to be able to thank the lady for her kindness in taking us in, for I'm sure that she had done her best in her own way.

We found the door open and no-one at home except the two older Chihuahuas, who snarled and showed displeasure at our intrusion, eyeing us suspiciously. There was nothing for it but to start fastening our suitcases, and prepare to leave, trusting she would return at any minute. I added a few words to the note making apologies for not seeing her – but would call to explain later. We had reached the gate when the first air raid warning sounded, so very soon after that speech by the Prime Minister. It seemed to have a personal power to strike fear into us – the fear of the unknown: bombs, gas, invasion; we didn't know what to think.

My stomach turned to ice, frozen with fear that I tried to hide from my child. Quickly, I said, 'Let's get along to our new home.' So my exit was a rapid one, dragging Joy with one hand and two cases with the other. We had gone only a few steps, when a voice called, 'Hi! Come back. Where are you going?'

It was the good lady who obviously thought that we were absconding with the family silver under the cover of the air raid warning. She had been paying a call on a neighbour across the street and amazingly had not seen us returning. Hastily calling out that there was a note of explanation, we hurried on. The most urgent need now was to get under cover among friends – we couldn't wait, expecting bombs to fall any minute.

Breathlessly, we stumbled to our leader's lodgings. The kindly soul, whose acquaintance I had made earlier on, made us a cup of tea and calmed us. She didn't appear to be a bit perturbed and it wasn't long before we all breathed easy again as the All Clear sounded. Only then did we know it to have been a false alarm.

Not long after, we were introduced to the two ladies who had kindly consented to house us: a Mrs and Miss Gibbs. They were delightful people – very special. I shall never forget the kindness and understanding that they showed to us. They did their best to make us welcome and happy. [Editor's note: Mrs and Miss Gibbs were probably a widow and her sister-in-law. Their house, in Queen's Road, Tankerton, was called Strathbrook.]

No sooner had we arrived than they set about preparing a very good meal, which was very much appreciated by the both of us. All the while, they talked to us, taking a lively interest in our affairs. They couldn't have been kinder had they been relations. I was finally able to write and post a letter to Tom, telling him our new address, and how thankful we were to be with such good people. I still had no idea where he was and had no way of finding out.

Our rising spirits were shattered when, the very next day, the British liner *Athenia* was sunk by a submarine. This act of cruelty inflamed public feeling and all were glad to hear that the RAF had raided the Kiel Canal entrance and sunk German warships.

6

SETTLING DOWN

he next important task was to work out a routine for the children. Schools had not
commenced the autumn term and, in any case, so many locals had gone away. It would
appear to be a few weeks before education could be organised officially, and our evacuees
could not be left all day at the homes of their new foster parents – that would certainly have
caused complaints. Indeed, they would need some respite from the unusual conditions they
now found themselves in. Having children around was a new experience to some of these kind
people, and I think some must have found it pretty exhausting. Even the best of children can be
a disturbing influence and can also cause distress to those unaccustomed to them.

So we had to do something to make each day as interesting and happy as possible for our
little groups. The beach was a great draw but, at the time, much of it had been closed off
with barbed wire defences. We helped them write letters to home and, in some cases, ask for
necessary items of clothing to be sent. Some luckier ones had been almost reclothed by the

TANKERTON SLOPES, WHITSTABLE.   20

The seafront at Tankerton and the famous slopes in the 1930s.

A typical Whitstable scene after anti-invasion measures had been taken. At Tankerton, the barbed wire was installed at the top of the Slopes, as well as in lengths along the beach. *(Photograph courtesy of Messenger Group Newspapers)*

wealthier householders with whom they now lodged, and one lady offered me several pairs of shoes for needy little ones. These had been left by her summer visitors and she was happy to find that they could be well used.

Those donated shoes would soon prove to very useful indeed. Three children all from one family, one boy and two girls, had obviously come from a very poor home and the youngest, about six years old, seemed to be forever grizzling. As we sat on a clear stretch of the beach, I began fitting the shoes where needed, and all three of the little family were wearing Wellingtons. I remarked that it was surely too hot to be wearing them – why hadn't they worn shoes? As it turned out, none of them had any shoes, and the tiny one, still crying, couldn't get hers off. Then I found out to my dismay that her Wellingtons were two sizes too small for her and on the wrong feet. No wonder she was miserable; no wonder she cried and cried. We finally managed to get them off and tried a nice pair of sandals and that fitted perfectly. I chaffed the poor little feet to get life back into them, noting the threadbare socks. That was another thing we must get, I noted to myself.

The poor little girl with the sore feet soon began to smile again, and put her skeleton arms – like signposts of winter – around my neck, so delighted with her new shoes and her newly found comfort. It later transpired that her older sister had been expected to see to her washing and dressing, and her temporary foster mother was horrified at our findings. She had three children of her own, but after things had been adjusted, the strangers happily integrated with the poor but loving Tankerton family.

On our various perambulations round the shops and houses, I met and made friends with many of the local residents, and many would stop and ask how we were all getting on. Many of them offered items of clothing and, on some occasions, picture books for the evacuees. As expected, these gifts were very welcome indeed.

We took groups to a Nonconformist church on Sundays for morning service and afternoon Sunday School, where they learnt to sing jolly little choruses that were both lively and tuneful, and they all thoroughly enjoyed it. The congregation in the mornings was 90 per cent elderly ladies, and very few local children, for in that particular locality, there were few young families with children. One old gentleman stopped us and told me that it was refreshing to see some young blood about the place. We also made the acquaintance of the pastor and his wife; they were a very devout couple and, because of the evacuees, I was in constant touch with them. [Editor's note: The church in question was the Tankerton Free Church in Northwood Road,

Part of the main shopping thoroughfare in Tankerton; this particular scene being dominated by the premises of George Fitt Motors Ltd.

Jessie (left) and Joy (front right) with Mrs Williams, and one of her daughters, in the back garden of their St Anne's Road house.

Ivy Hookham (front row, third from right) with other volunteers outside the Red Cross station in Cromwell Road, Whitstable. Dr Barker is centre-right. Today, the building is St Peter's Church Hall.

Ivy, in full SRN uniform, outside the front door of their Ellis Road house.

between the junctions for Wynn Road and Manor Road. In harness at the time was the Revd Mr Williams, who was a strict Puritan. Having found out that Jessie had taken Joy to see *In Which We Serve*, he preached that it was sinful to go to the cinema, constantly training his eyes on them both as he spoke. By contrast, Mrs Williams was warm and friendly, and my grandmother soon struck up a friendship with her. In fact, Mrs Williams became a welcome shoulder for her to cry on when she heard from the evil propagandist Lord Haw-Haw that Tom's ship had been sunk by the German Navy; a lie broadcast no less than three times. Joy also became pals with the two Williams' daughters: Muriel and, we think, Susan.]

Some of my charges were still feeling homesick and people were having quite a lot of trouble with tears, tantrums and bed-wetting, as a result of the upheaval in their lives – an inevitable reaction to their otherwise uneventful routine. On the whole though, people tried to be understanding about it all and tolerated the trials and the wet beds. In most cases, these good folk had my sincere respect for they were willingly doing their bit for the war effort. Some kiddies were extremely fortunate finding themselves in luxury homes that they'd never ever dreamt of: well fed, well shod and well cared for; the people making every endeavour to be as mothers to them.

Some children, of course, were ungrateful little beggars, but given the perversity of human nature, they couldn't all be good all of the time. Those of us in nominal charge made excuses for them – the trauma of war, being away from parents, etc. We also did our best to lecture the miscreants and ask them to do better. Indeed, these troublesome children improved with time, and it wasn't long before they were all behaving as well as could be expected.

Our greatest scourge was the presence of head lice on some of the evacuees, and it was a source of great worry and, it has to be admitted, disgust among some of the residents, who had hardly heard of such things, much less seen them. Luckily, help was at hand. We quickly rounded up the afflicted ones, during the first few days, and herded them off to the clinic for treatment.

 By this time, the authorities had discovered that my sister-in-law, Ivy Hookham, was a state-registered nurse, and she was literally pounced upon to take on duties at the local clinic. Ivy happily gave her services voluntarily, producing her uniform that had been packed away since her practising days. She did sterling work, making a great contribution to the war effort by performing district nurse duties. She later moved house from the Medway towns to the area; she brought a little motorcycle and became quite a well-known figure as she moved from place to place. [Editor's note: Ivy Hookham, with her young son Bob, had been evacuated from City Way, Rochester, at the same time as Jessie and Joy and were billeted with a Congregational Minister in Baddlesmere Road, Tankerton, for a short period. The Hookhams then rented a house at no. 15 Ellis Road, also in Tankerton.]

7

LILY

One little girl in our group proved to be an enigma – a very real worry. No-one wanted her because of her general appearance. On the first day, she had started off on the journey with the dirtiest, shabbiest dress, devoid of buttons, no socks, and dirty plimsolls on her feet. Her hair, which showed signs that it might at one time have been curly, hung in greasy rat-tails to her shoulders. She was called Lily and I thought of the purity of that beautiful flower and the image that the very name brought to me, and I wondered what sort of a person could let a child get into that state? What was the child's mother thinking of, to let her join a group, with hardly any possessions – just the barest of necessities packed in a carrier bag? Overriding all was the penetrating acrid smell that came from the child's underwear – she definitely needed a change of knickers!

Part of Tankerton seafront, and the famous Slopes, in their heyday between the wars. Note the tiered rows of beach huts.

Lily was an outgoing, friendly little girl, with a ready smile and a great sense of fun, but on that first day, no-one showed the least sign of wanting her. Sometimes, she would lower her long lashes, and one was left wondering what went on behind them. The eyes are the windows of the soul, and they might have told us much. She talked freely of her Gran, so one gathered that her mother didn't figure in her life very much. We had the impression that this nine-year-old girl had seen more in her short life than the average child would see in a lifetime.

After two attempts to house her satisfactorily, we found two kindly spinsters – sisters who appeared to have come straight out of a Dickens novel. They were both delightfully old-fashioned in their mode of dress and hairstyle and very devout in their way of life (the Revd Williams would certainly have approved of them!). Having been told about Lily, the story touched the hearts of these kindly sisters, and they offered her a home. This must have been a turning point in Lily's life, and I venture to suggest that she would have, in time, turned out to be quite a little lady, unless, of course, she returned to her old life. Sadly, this we shall never know, because all too soon, upon the fall of Europe under the Nazi jackboot, most of the evacuees were moved back out of the district – some by parents and some by the authorities – and we never saw or heard of them again. In the meantime though, while she was in our care, we saw the little waif take on an entirely different way of life. The two dear old ladies must have sat up all night to make the clothes in which they dressed the child and the style was distinctly 'retro' compared with the other children. Much shampooing and brushing had brought out the lost beauty of her hair, and her face was like a well-scrubbed carrot, and lit up with love given to her by her two Victorian benefactors.

Lily's coarse dialect gradually faded away and, one way or another, I thought of her as a junior *Pygmalion*: like Eliza Doolittle, the character created by George Bernard Shaw.

The two ladies had every reason to be proud of their handiwork, but there was one thing that worried them. Although they had coaxed Lily to write home, it was weeks before she

Joy (left) with the two Williams sisters, Muriel and Susan (?), on a section of the beach at Tankerton that was free of anti-invasion defences.

finally heard back from her mother. The child's mother had been invited to come on a visit, and eventually we were told by a proud and excited Lily that her Mum would be coming down on the following Sunday. We were all, quite naturally, very interested to see what she looked like, but judging by Lily's appearance in the early days, we were not expecting very much out of the ordinary.

Imagine our surprise then, when Lily took her mother along to see our group leader. I happened to be there at the time and could hardly believe my eyes. My first impression was, 'she's a cool one!' The vision I beheld was in the height of fashion, with sheer silk stockings and high-heeled shoes, and a cute little hat perched on top of a carefully arranged mop of hair. In fact, the only thing that matched up with Lily was the flaming red hair. She had a fur necklet slung nonchalantly round her shoulders and sparklers dangled from her ears, and more at her low-cut blouse.

If we were surprised at Lily's mother, how much more surprised might she have been at the sight of her daughter, as she had never seen her before! Apparently, she accepted the hospitality of the elderly ladies, who had worked miracles with her daughter, had a good meal with them, and then took herself off at about 4.30 p.m. without a word of thanks.

8

BLACKOUT JOURNEY

One week had passed since war had been declared, and we had settled in well. The schools were to open at last and we were looking forward to getting the evacuees incorporated into them with the remaining local children.

Joy and I were still worrying and waiting to hear from Tom, but we had to try to understand that letters were going to be difficult from now on. The days passed away easily enough, but the nights seemed endless – sleep would not come because of the anxieties.

On one particular Saturday night, Joy and I went to bed as usual, in the comfortable bedroom that Mrs Gibbs had given us and, for the first time in a week, I quickly drifted into a troubled sleep. At sometime between two and three in the early hours, I woke, hearing a muffled knock at the front door below. I wasn't much disturbed, thinking its was none of my business, and so turned over comfortably to continue the precious sleep I so badly needed. But it wasn't to be this time, so I lay there staring at the ceiling, hoping that the morning light would come quickly, and the day's activities fill my mind.

After a while, voices drifted upwards – a man's deep voice, and hurrying to the landing, I knew directly that it was Tom. But how, why, where? All these questions flashed through my mind as I almost flew down the stairs and into his arms. At first, I thought I must be dreaming, but that familiar smell of tobacco, the carbolic soap, that shipboard aroma so familiar to me, all reassured me that I wasn't. It was Tom alright. Suddenly, there was so much that I wanted to know.

Those two old darlings, in whose house we now lodged, did not have any objections to being raised from their sleep in the middle of the night; they knew what it meant to us. They went into the kitchen at that early hour to make a meal for him. Tom protested, with much thanks, that he didn't want to give any trouble. He was only too thankful that he had found us, but they insisted that he must have something to eat, especially when they heard that he had been travelling most of the day and night.

Tom was so choked with emotion that he found it difficult to swallow the food. Our good friends wanted to make up a bed for him, but we insisted that they must not bother. We were only too pleased to cuddle up in the same bed. The two of us had so much to say, and there were so many questions to be asked and the time was too precious to waste in sleep.

It appeared that HMS *Vindictive* had put in at Rosyth and then proceeded to Portsmouth for paying off. Tom had a short weekend leave, so he made his way to London by rail, by which time it was late evening and dark as pitch with the blackout in force everywhere. Leaving the station with three other servicemen, who had travelled on the same train, they kept together

The oldest railway bridge in the world, carrying the Canterbury to Whitstable Railway over the appropriately named Old Bridge Road. The main line to Thanet, and the approach to Whitstable station itself, is just out of sight to the left.

Whitstable High Street between the wars: a scene that has changed little today, apart from the traffic!

in order to hire a taxi, as the last train down to Kent had gone. It wasn't easy to find one, for as soon as the destination was known, they were refused. At last, they found a driver who, although reluctant at first, saw their plight and relented. The four travellers almost begged the little Cockney and, by pooling their resources, made him a handsome offer to do the long journey to East Kent.

My husband and his companions, hitherto unknown to each other, were now comrades in adversity. They could very well understand the driver's reluctance to undertake such a journey in such conditions. The night was pitch black, made worse by the regulated blackouts, and the taxi driver admitted that he didn't really know the way. Moreover, without any signposts to guide him, the prospect was somewhat daunting. All signposts had been removed just prior to the outbreak of war, in order to thwart possible spies.

A London cabbie is a very special type: friendly and out going, and on this occasion, he was doing a good turn, which the four servicemen greatly appreciated. One man was heading for Chatham and another a few miles on, and the other wanted Ramsgate. And so they left London for Thanet, a bad enough journey in the dark at any time, but in the intense darkness of wartime conditions, it was positively dangerous. Luckily, the cabbie was a plucky little fellow, and so with all four passengers peering into the darkness, they eventually reached Chatham and offloaded one. So far so good.

The rest of the journey was something of a nightmare, with the remaining three trying to identify familiar landmarks that showed up only dimly. Eventually, Tom was dropped off in the middle of Whitstable's main street. He had never been there before and hadn't the faintest idea which way to turn. Somewhere not far away, his wife and daughter were sleeping, but he didn't know how to find them. He groped his way along the pavement until wild thoughts filled his mind. Was he walking in the wrong direction? There was no way of knowing. There's a blackout, and it's the middle of the night, he thought; better stand still for a while and think.

At that moment, a bulky figure bumped into him: it was a friendly policeman doing his nightly beat of the shops and houses in the area. When he heard Tom's plight, he said, 'don't worry chum – I'm on my way in your direction. Come along with me!' Those words almost sounded like an arrest, but Tom was very pleased to be 'arrested' in this way; it was like music to his ears, and so they walked onward together chatting like old friends. Tom would have liked to have met that man afterwards, but he never saw his face. It is also to be wondered how that 'good Samaritan' taxi driver made it back to London? We hope he completed his journey with no mishaps.

After about 25 minutes' walking, the bobby brought Tom right to the gate, and the rest I have already related. There was not much of the night left and Tom and I made our plans for the future; plans that envisaged us remaining in the Whitstable area after the horrors of war had passed. All the while, our little one was blissfully sleeping, unaware that her Daddy was so near. What a surprise she would have in the morning! [Editor's note: My mother recalls a far-less idyllic reunion. So that my grandparents could be alone together for the few hours they had, Joy was packed off to a neighbour's house. Unfortunately, she found this strange new place rather dark and forbidding, so screamed the place down, and wouldn't be placated until she'd been returned to the Gibbs' Queen's Road house. My mother spent the rest of the night sleeping between her parents, thus completely spoiling their night of passion.]

9

A HOME OF OUR OWN

Having discussed the matter with Tom in the few hours we had together during his short weekend leave, we both decided that it was imperative to get a home together in the area. First of all, we must look around and find a little house, and that was the task that we had in hand on that Sunday morning. In this endeavour, we were quite overwhelmed by the kindness of the two Gibbs ladies who, not only provided a very nice breakfast for the three of us – all sitting at the table happily and making us feel so much a part of their family – but also, helped us by advising where to look for a suitable place to rent.

Many people had departed from the area already and left everything behind them, just as we had in Rochester. In fact, during the previous week, I had several people offer me the run of their homes, while they were away, only to keep them from the depreciation that inevitably sets in with an empty building. Rent free, they said, but although it seemed a tempting offer at first, we decided that we wanted a home of our own that, God willing, Tom could come home to again. The twists and turns of fate had brought us to Whitstable and we planned to put our roots down and stay.

In a short time, we had found just what we needed in a nice road that suited us very well – just two up and two down, with kitchen, bathroom and garden. [Editor's note: This house was at no. 61 Wynn Road, Tankerton, only a stone's throw from the Gibbs' house, the Free Church, and all the other connections that my grandmother had already made.]

Tom and I were given the address of the owner by the lady next door, which she did with a kindly smile, looking at the big man in his smart Navy uniform and gas mask slung over his shoulder. I instantly knew that she would approve of us as neighbours, and I took an instinctive liking to her as well. We hurried off again to a house opposite the Whitstable railway station, about 1½ miles away, and met an amiable old couple who were only too pleased to let the house at a reasonable rent. We paid in advance, and took the key and the rent-book, happy that we had taken a wise step.

Back with our wonderful landladies, we were treated to an excellent meal, and they even said they were proud to be entertaining a sailor. I was proud of him also: a fine looking man, robust and of equable temperament – not like some people's idea of a sailor, a brash, hard drinking, hard-swearing son-of-a-gun, jolly jack tar type. He was none of these things, being quietly spoken, gentle and kind. On top of that, his Methodist heritage ensured a teetotal lifestyle, which was uncharacteristic of many in his chosen career. However, what endeared him to most people, and still did throughout his life, was his intense desire to please and never offend in any way.

Settling in at no. 61 Wynn Road. Jessie
sews a patchwork quilt, no doubt while
thinking of Tom.

Tom Vine (back row, second from right)
and other officers of the Chatham
Gunnery School, during the 'Phoney
War'.

Sadly, Tom went back that evening, but we could at least be satisfied that we'd achieved a lot in those all-too-short sixteen hours together. The very next morning, I was excused from duties by our leader; fortunately my presence was not urgently needed. Leaving Joy in the care of our two benevolent ladies, I went back to Rochester to look for a removal firm. This was not a very easy task to achieve at the time, for so many people were moving to other places, which they hoped would be safe. Fortunately I had success at last and left the key of my bungalow with them, trusting to their honesty and good nature to bring everything to the new Tankerton address. If you recall the time of our departure, nothing had been packed, as indeed it would have been under different circumstances.

Luckily, nothing went amiss, and I spent much of the following few days getting straight at no. 61, and making our new house look like a home.

Meanwhile, Tom's ship had been paid off at Portsmouth and he had transferred to Chatham Gunnery School – assigned to the parade ground, taking charge of the intake of 'hostilities only' classes, new from Civvy Street: all types from all backgrounds, and he had to get them into shape.

When Tom could manage it, he came home; like all servicemen, heeding instructions to be within recall distance. Joy would watch closely for his arrival, and I allowed her to stand at the end of the road, within sight both ways, and immediately she spotted his familiar figure striding down the road, she would run to meet him, leaping into his arms to be carried home.

Back in the house, Joy ransacked his pockets to find the packet of Smarties, or the chocolate bar, which she knew would be there. Some of Tom's friends gave him their unwanted sweet ration for his little girl, and she always made the most of them, making them last by biting each Smartie in half. The war up to this moment had affected us very little, except for the shortages, which were getting worse each week, as housewives gradually found new ways to adapt.

By now, the evacuees were all doing well at school, and were quite used to their new lives. Having said that, the evacuation had lasted longer than anyone had anticipated and some

parents had recalled their children. This period of relative quiet and complacency was known as 'the Phoney War'. Apart from keeping in touch with the children, and looking after them at weekends, my duties were not at all arduous. By this time, Joy had a welcome little companion in the house, for I had taken in a little girl evacuee to live with us. She was a well-brought-up child and as pretty as picture. Her name was June and Joy adored her. [Editor's note: The evacuee's name was June Shave and she had come down from London. As it turned out, June's stay in Tankerton was short-lived and, as the events of 1940 took on an increasingly darker shade, her mother came to collect her.]

Evacuee June Shave, with Joy, on a family walk along South Street in the winter of 1939/40.

Settling in at no. 61 Wynn Road. Joy
tries out her old swing, shortly after
it had been moved down from the
Rochester house.

When weather permitted, we spent much of our time on the beach, before they closed it off completely, and life passed by pleasantly enough. One day, we saw a yellow object floating on the tide, and I swam out to capture it. I might mention that it was not too far out, thank goodness, as swimming is not one of my strong points. It proved to be a lemon, probably dropped from a passing ship, but sad to say it was thoroughly waterlogged and useless. However, we kept it for some time as a relic of what used to be.

If the weather was bad, I often rounded up the children and, rather than let them roam the streets, I'd have them in my house just to relieve their foster parents for brief spells. On these occasions, we were a hive of activity, making little paper models, and having games or lessons. I would clear away all ornaments and give them the run of the house downstairs, and it kept them happy. The evacuees were pleased with this arrangement, considering all things, for they knew that I would produce goodies that I had baked the previous day, for good behaviour of course.

All through this time, we were rationed, but people were very kind and good to these children. They loved singing 'We're gonna hang out the washing on the Siegfried Line', without knowing what it was all about.

All too soon though, the children were to know a lot more.

10

AT THE TIME OF DUNKIRK

Early 1940, and things were still relatively quiet on the home front. The sea froze at Whitstable, but nothing else remarkable happened. However, overseas, suffering was the lot of thousands of people. The headlines of our newspapers became daily more horrific. Warsaw, followed by Denmark, and then Norway; all were annexed by Hitler, that wicked and arrogant man who was flourishing.

Britain was numbed and shocked by the news of HMS *Royal Oak* being sunk at Scapa Flow, with 818 lives lost. What audacity to sink her in home waters! Hitler had no compassion for the sorrow and suffering that he was causing in the world. In fact, he was ready and eager for more conquests, and confident of his success in this endeavour. Inevitably, more countries were overrun: Holland, then little Luxembourg, and then Belgium. When would there be retribution? We wanted vengeance on the Nazi tyrant who was terrorising the world. So many people, by now, were badly shaken – but were greatly heartened when, on 11 May, Winston Churchill formed a National Government.

Looking towards Whitstable Harbour, across the frozen seashore, 23 January 1940.

Tom spending a valued weekend break with his family, in the back garden of no. 61 Wynn Road, during spring 1940.

Churchill was a fine example and inspiration to the British people, uplifting our hearts and rekindling our hope. We all knew that, at last, we had a real leader and our faith in him was paramount. His picture, with the ubiquitous cigar, seemed to appear in books, papers and on posters everywhere, and this was a great morale-booster to us all.

On 13 May, Queen Wilhelmina of the Netherlands came to London for sanctuary. Events were hotting up further and faster than we'd ever thought possible.

Then came Dunkirk from 27 May to 4 June. The very name brings back a host of agonising memories. The event has been recorded graphically by those who were there – it has been shown on film and the blow was great. The awful memory of the appalling loss of life and the extreme bravery of 335,498 officers and men who were evacuated from a living hell, still fills us with pride, and also admiration for their gallant rescuers. There were 428 warships and numerous other vessels – the little craft of men with stout hearts who came from all ports to take part in the epic rescue, under constant attack from a ruthless enemy, leaving many dead on the beaches.

Mercifully, at least the elements were not against them, for the weather conditions were marvellous. The rescued men, in various conditions, were entrained at all ports around the coast, and some of those brave troops passed through our district along the railway from Ramsgate. In the bright sunshine, neighbours came down to cheer them on their way.

Those grimy war-scarred heroes were full of British pluck, gratefully accepting jugs of tea, which we handed up to them in the carriages when the trains slowed down. Teacups, teapots, plates of cake and precious cigarettes were eagerly hauled in. Nothing was too good for those returning soldiers, and the loss of the crockery, as it was whisked away to London, was nothing to the pride that we felt for this heart-stirring situation. [Editor's note: I remember my grandmother telling me that many folk from Tankerton lined the railway, all the way from the foot crossing on the path from Queen's Road to Ham Shades Lane, right down to the Castle Road overbridge near to Whitstable station. This was how Jessie managed to lose an entire tea service, as she attempted to refresh these poor rescued men.]

From that moment on, the fear of invasion hung over us, and while we sat on the bank waiting for the next trainload for us to cheer on their way, I was expecting that my husband might possibly arrive home for the weekend, as his duties were still at the Chatham Gunnery School. Consequently, I was continually looking towards the railway station, in the hope of seeing his familiar figure come striding along, but there was no sign of him.

When we went back home, Joy took up her usual vantage point at the end of Wynn Road, in order to glance up Queen's Road and watch for her Daddy to appear in the distance. At one point, she looked back at me with concern.

'I can see a man in the distance, but it's not Daddy,' she said. I immediately joined her at the junction.

'Is it not? Look again . . . I believe it is!' But why is he walking so slowly, I thought to myself; why isn't he bounding along at his usual pace?

We both hurried to him as he came nearer, and we could soon see that he was in trouble. He said he had great pains in his stomach and wanted to get indoors as soon as possible. How he achieved that journey from the railway station to the house, I'll never know, but once inside, he collapsed, and my kind neighbour hurried to fetch the doctor. Fortunately, he came promptly and diagnosed appendicitis. The doctor quickly alerted the nearest hospital, only to be told that they couldn't accept Naval personnel – he would have to be taken back to the Naval hospital in Chatham – he belonged to the Royal Navy.

Following a telephone call by the doctor, arrangements were made for an RN ambulance to fetch him, as soon as possible. The night went on seemingly endlessly and the pain got worse and worse. When I asked him why he hadn't reported sick at the barracks, he said that he didn't want to miss his time at home with us. Any time might be the last before he had to go away.

As the night dragged on, he was in a heavy sweat, with violent pain and was clearly in a bad way. I was beside myself with worry, and still no ambulance turned up. As dawn came, we were still waiting. And then, at last, at about six o'clock, a Royal Navy ambulance, staffed by two men, arrived to take him away. They had received many calls during the night, as there'd been a raid on Chatham, and they just couldn't have come any earlier. By this time, Tom hardly knew me, but was able to say, 'don't worry,' when I kissed him goodbye. Those two strong men then had a hefty task lifting a 13-stone man down that narrow stairway.

Hours of anxiety followed before I could contact the hospital, only for me to hear, to my dismay, that Tom had just arrived in time. It was a severe case of peritonitis, which had burst at the onset of the operation. Luckily, his robust constitution stood him in good stead, and he made a good recovery.

Despite the raids, I was able to make my way to the hospital 'somewhere in Kent'. Being so frantic with worry, I cannot recall where, or how, I got there, but I finally saw him, sitting in a chair, dressed in hospital blue. What a relief it was to see a smiling Tom again.

During his recuperation, he was given a fairly quiet job in the Gunnery Office, and continued, on occasions, to make his way home to us, as work permitted. By now, Tom was a Chief Petty Officer. It was also at this time that most of the evacuees departed for other places.

I I

OFF TO WAR

J oy and I were convinced that Tom would be assigned to a ship very soon, and those happy days of having him close at hand, and also safe, would come to an end. And so it proved to be. He began a new job in the spring of 1941: organising the gunnery department of a brand new ship built at Chatham. It was called HMS *Euryalus* (God of the open sea), a cruiser of the 'Dido' Class, which all had Greek names, including *Hermione, Dido, Naiad, Cleopatra* and *Sirius*. These ships would become known as the 'Fighting Fifteen', under Admiral Vian, of Cossack fame.

That sneering Haw-Haw on the German radio said, 'The *Euryalus* will never sail.' However, on 26 June 1941, the ship's company of the new cruiser were on the quarterdeck to ask a blessing of God on their ship, which was about to set sail. Captain Eric Bush repeated the ancient bidding, 'That we may be worthy of the trust committed to our charge . . . what do we fear if God is with us?'

HMS *Euryalus*, Tom's new ship, in the summer of 1942, shortly after being commissioned.

Tom meets his older brother Jim aboard HMS *Euryalus*, while docked at Alexandria, some time during 1942.

'We fear nothing!' the company responded.

After the working-up period, the *Euryalus* was ready for sea. The first journey was part of a convoy to Gibraltar and then on to Malta, covering the main convoy until they were taken over by another squadron. And then, there would be the return to Gibraltar, on to South Africa, up to the west coast of Africa and through the Suez Canal to Alexandria.

It was a happy ship and the men had every confidence in and great respect for their skipper. Alexandria became their base in May 1942 and from there, they did Malta convoys, shipping sweeps and work with the Eighth Army in bombarding the North Africa coast. [Editor's note: In Alexandria, Tom would be reunited with his older brother Jim, who had emigrated to South Africa some years before, and had joined the army as a war correspondent for a large Cape Town-based newspaper.]

Of course, I knew nothing of these movements until after the war. The anguish of being a serviceman's wife in wartime is not knowing where her man is, how he is faring, or even if he is still alive. Letters from Tom came in dribs and drabs, with no information in them whatsoever for they were all censored. A few sailors' wives in the district contacted each other when mail arrived, to compare notes in an effort to glean a speck of real interest, even though our husbands were on different ships. One wife that I knew lived at the far end of Whitstable, but she would push her child – a little boy called 'Ronnie Wriggle' – in the pram, all the way to our house to see if I had received a letter too. [Editor's note: Ronnie was the son of Mr and Mrs Revell, and it is thought that they were part of a larger Whitstable-based family. In fact, my

Jessie reading a welcome letter from Tom, 'somewhere in the Mediterranean'.

grandfather, Mr Revell and another Navy man called Ted (?) Garrett – who also lived in Wynn Road – were known locally as 'The Three Musketeers' as they would nearly always travel home from sea together.]

There was a great deal of comradeship among wives as well as among men, and I am sure that both husbands and wives really felt those words of the hymn, 'Keep our loved ones now far distant, 'neath Thy care'.

The Nazi propaganda machine continued its onslaught, trying to intimidate the British public. That traitor Lord Haw-Haw was at it again, sneering and contemptuous, becoming a nasty part of our lives. He was continually reporting the loss of British shipping, sometimes both unfortunately and uncomfortably close to the truth. Many times though, it was false information, and underlying it, the hatred always showed through. Often, I heard that the *Euryalus* had gone down. It was all intended to shatter the morale of us at home, but we knew that we had to keep faith. There was nothing else that we could do but go on hoping and praying, and this went on for over two years in our case.

All the while, the *Euryalus* was experiencing torpedo bombers, dive-bombing Stukas, U-boat attacks and mines, besides the Italian fleet, which was a far superior force and included the *Littoria*, a 15in-gun battleship.

Everything was against a ship at sea, especially if they had no air cover, as was the case with the *Euryalus*, and yet the enemy had air bases all around. Luckily, *Euryalus* seemed to have a charmed life, taking everything that the enemy could throw at her, while watching other ships in the convoy being sunk, and she was able to keep going despite many near misses and the consequent damage sustained. She was straddled by the Italian guns and splintered by large chunks penetrating the superstructure. The paint was burned off the guns through continual use. Their sister ship, HMS *Cleopatra*, just ahead, was hit by a 6in shell on the bridge, but managed to keep going. Men under pressure became fatalists, 'If it's to come, may it be quick.' Captain Eric Bush of the *Euryalus* was a man of courage, and when in the heat of action, with death virtually staring him in the face, he kept as cool as a cucumber. As such, he won the sincere admiration of all his men.

Of all Tom's duties, the Malta convoys were the main concern, as food, fuel and ammunition had to be got through to the starving people of that little island. One particular action in achieving that goal was known as the 'David and Goliath Battle', because the odds were so stacked against them. On this occasion, the Italian battleships, superior in armaments, were routed by the British – it was described as trying to match cannon with popguns. In the end, Malta received her supplies, which were so necessary to the defence of her homeland.

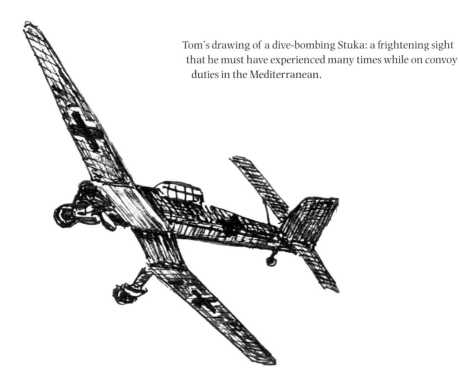

Tom's drawing of a dive-bombing Stuka: a frightening sight that he must have experienced many times while on convoy duties in the Mediterranean.

Addressing the ship's company, the captain emphasised the importance of the achievement in getting the convoy through, saying that they saved hundreds, if not thousands of lives. On their way back to base in Alexandria, the ship spent twelve hours of daylight in bomb alley, so called because of having no air cover. The guns of the *Euryalus* were rusty that day, the paint having peeled off them.

In the aftermath, the following message was sent by Sir Winston Churchill to the Commander-in-Chief of the Mediterranean Fleet, Admiral Sir Andrew Cunningham:

> I shall be glad if you will convey to Admiral Vian, and all who sailed with him, the admiration which I feel at this resolute and brilliant action by which the Malta convoy was saved. That one of the most powerful modern battleships afloat, attended by four cruisers and a flotilla, should have been routed and put to flight with severe torpedo injury in broad daylight by a force of five British light cruisers and destroyers, constitutes a Naval episode of the highest distinction and entitles all ranks and ratings concerned, and above all their Commander, to the compliments of the British nation.

On another convoy, during a critical stage after fighting through with supplies to Malta, as the *Euryalus* came into the Grand Harbour, it seemed that all the people had turned out, lining the terraces and cheering the ships in. It must have been an impressive sight, and heartening to the people, to see those battle-scarred ships limping into harbour.

HMS *Euryalus* stayed on over a period as guard ship and then covered the landings at Sicily and Salerno, working with the Eighth Army tank concentrations. [Editor's note: Further details of HMS *Euryalus*' wartime operations can be found as the appendix to this book.]

12

NEIGHBOURS & RATIONS

From the late summer of 1940 onwards, our lives were being disrupted by daylight raids although, in Whitstable, we were on the fringe rather than in the thick of it. We saw dogfights overhead and also observed huge formations of German bombers going over to lay waste to the big cities, in particular London, and we very often received some backlash as the Dorniers jettisoned explosives when returning to occupied Europe.

All throughout this time, people were very good to each other. In adversity, the very best in humanity comes to the fore. On one particular occasion, we had been shopping in Whitstable High Street when, on the return trip, the air raid warning sounded. For a moment, we were frozen in fear. Luckily, a nearby door opened and a young woman called, 'come in quickly!' Joy and I went into the house and were introduced to her invalid mother, who was already sheltering under the stairs. We had sat there together chatting for a long time, when they decided to have their meal and invited us to join in. I really appreciated the gesture, but was hesitant to eat other people's rations, but they insisted and with a little more cabbage, and a little more carrot, the stew was stretched to four. I thought that was a real kindness and, on top of that, I had made two more friends.

Back in Tankerton, I felt particularly blessed to find that my Wynn Road neighbours were such nice people. Mrs Taylor took me under her wing and was very kind. She was also a great comfort when distress came over the airwaves – Haw-Haw stopped at nothing, he went on relentlessly. Mrs T. would gladly mind Joy if I had anything special to do and every afternoon, without fail, she or her husband would hand a cup of tea to me over the garden fence. It was heartening to know that someone was interested in my comings and goings. By contrast to his wife, Mr Taylor was a taciturn character, handing me a cuppa with just a nod of the head. He hardly ever smiled and seldom ever spoke, but when he did, it was with some pearl of wit that always surprised me. In any case, I figured that such an uncommunicative man must surely be difficult to live with.

We all 'dug for victory' in our small back gardens. Even Joy helped with her little spade. I began with planting shallots because I couldn't buy onion seed or sets. I also sowed carrots, beans, beet and marrows, and met with quite a good success rate for a novice.

Mr Taylor was usually there to ask advice and, on one occasion, when I had dug the drills and was popping in the seed potatoes, he said, 'you'll alter all those little spuds doin' that,' and thinking I was doing it all wrong, asked 'why?' He replied with a grin, 'because they'll grow into big 'uns!' That was his kind of joke, but he was always very good to me, often sharing this-and-that to help fill the garden.

Joy watering the freshly sown vegetable seeds at Wynn Road, as carrots and shallots replaced the usual bedding plants.

Jessie and Joy proudly harvest their first crop of 'Dig for Victory' tomatoes in the front garden. Joy cannot help but take a quick sample of the produce!

Instead of the wee patch in the front of the house being bright with flowers, we felt it was patriotic to plant tomatoes. In fact, I grew some very fine specimens and felt highly delighted when they were admired by passers-by. One young neighbour told me that she had been advised to empty the contents of her child's potty on her tomatoes, and whether she took the advice or not I never knew, but I didn't much care for the idea myself. [Editor's note: When my grandmother described her front garden as a 'wee patch', I thought she'd meant that it was small!] My own good crop of tomatoes was the result of tipping the washing-up water on it and we were soon proudly eating our own home-growns.

Rationing did not start in real earnest until five months after the beginning of the war, and then suddenly everything was scarce – cheese, butter, sugar, milk and other essentials – but it is amazing what can be done with a little enterprise. Joy and I had the minimum rations, but we kept very healthy and no-one really suffered from the shortages. Looking back to those days of make-do, from the present time of plenty and even surpluses, I'm certain that it was good to be lean rather than overweight.

Cousins Bob Hookham and Joy Vine, during one of the long tricycle rides to Tyler Hill, in order to collect sweet chestnuts.

I regularly followed the 'Patsy' recipes in the newspaper, in the form of a strip cartoon. These depicted a girl supposedly cooking marvellous meals from the available supplies, and I kept those tips for years. Lord Woolton, Minister of Food, also gave us advice from time to time, such as how to use nettles for greens, camomile for tea, whale meat (which didn't please anybody) and toadstools called 'beef steak'. This was a fungus that could be found in the woods nearby, but we just could not force ourselves to try it. One of the advertised specialities was 'Woolton Pie', consisting of potatoes mixed with herbs and vegetables and topped with a pastry crust! At the time of writing, all of that sounds as if we had reached rock bottom, but we never thought this at the time.

In the late autumn, we had been able to cycle to the woods near Tyler Hill to gather chestnuts, which were plentiful that year. Joy and her cousin (Bob Hookham) had little red tricycles and we three would go to the woods and gather a lot of those lovely sweet chestnuts. There was practically no traffic about, so it was not at all dangerous taking them on the road with me. I made use of our woodland harvest in many ways, considering the chestnuts as a bonus in those days of shortages. They were a good thickener for soups and, cooked well and then minced, they made a sort of flour for pancakes and even cakes. At Christmas, a tolerably good 'almond paste' could also be concocted.

Christmas itself had to be very spartan, but we did the best we could. I'm afraid the pet rabbit, which hitherto had been led around the garden on a string, had to go for the pot, but we didn't enjoy it very much, because of Joy's remarks about 'poor Snowy'. On the plus side, there was a fruit allowance, so that humble mincemeat could be made and we also managed to make a cake of sorts. [Editor's note: Mince pies were one of my grandfather's seasonal favourites, but

The famous picture of 'Tom's favourite things', including a plate of mince pies, which was sent out to him in the Mediterranean.

not one he had a chance to indulge in on those gruelling Malta convoys. To cheer him up, my grandmother baked a batch of mince pies and then sent him a picture of them, together with other reminders of home, to give him something to look forward to when war was over.]

Eggs were very scarce and only appeared occasionally, sometimes two eggs in three weeks, and naturally they were more necessary for a growing child. I often longed for a nice newly-laid egg, but they didn't come our way. Therefore, when I heard that in some country villages one could get eggs served up for a meal, we made an effort and went out once. It was indeed a great effort and we did end up with two eggs each, but it never happened again. I suppose too many people heard about it.

We made good use of dried egg, although it had a taste rather like cardboard. We also had dried milk and not forgetting Spam (I wonder what that was made of!). Coffee was unobtainable and it was suggested that we try dandelion coffee. All I can say to that is 'Ugh!' but even that was not as bad as the Germans who, apparently, were drinking acorn coffee.

Pet owners found it difficult to feed their cats and dogs and so many of them 'disappeared'. A large family might have managed to find enough scraps if the pet wasn't too fussy, but with the meagre meat ration, it was almost impossible for elderly folk to keep a cherished pet, unless they sacrificed their own ration, which so many did. We often met and chatted to the lady with the Chihuahuas and it didn't look as if her little treasures went short of anything.

My little girl couldn't remember what a banana looked like and when we heard on the grapevine that there were some in the shops, we queued – and got one each! Oranges came very seldomly and, after all, it was the children who needed the vitamins. We were able to obtain orange juice, but we thought it was horrible stuff and I didn't know many children who liked it.

The sweet ration was always something to be looked forward to, for me as much as for Joy, because as soon as she got hers, it kept her good and out of trouble. She tried to make it last, but even with careful discipline, such a task was almost impossible for a small child. I only found out, many years later, that when my little girl did finally run out of sweets, she would go and stand by the front gate, with a much-practiced forlorn look on her face. Inevitably, a neighbour would notice and, in an effort to cheer the hapless child up, offer some of their own sweet ration to her. She was then full of thanks and much placated, which undoubtedly also did much to cheer the kindly donor too. How many times she pulled off this stunt, I can only guess at! It also helped Joy's cause that she was the only little girl at our end of Wynn Road.

Joy enjoys her sweet ration, while an envious 'friend' looks on.

A good spread at a Tankerton birthday party, especially considering the fact there was a war on.

Other more elaborate treats were unheard of and birthday parties for the kiddies seemed a thing of the past. Chocolate biscuits and jellies, iced buns and other fancies were no more, we thought, until one day, when I was asked to help out at an unexpected party. Joy had been invited and the event was anticipated with much speculation. On arrival, I gasped at the laden table, for there they were: all of the aforementioned forgotten treats. Some people certainly knew how to get things! [Editor's note: My mother still has fond memories of that party, which was for the birthday of her friend Anne Surman, who was a grocer's daughter. Her father had clearly been putting items by for several months in order to give the local children a special treat. The chocolate biscuits were a particularly notable delight.]

There were people in some trades who profited quite legally from wartime conditions, but many 'transactions' were illegal and came to be known as the black market. It cannot be denied that this existed quite extensively – tradesmen helping other tradesmen by exchanges in tit-for-tat fashion, and it was also recognised that some High Street traders were susceptible to feminine smiles.

13

NEIGHBOURS & SALVAGE

For a while, I knew very little about others in Wynn Road. As luck would have it, I heard that the local council wanted volunteers to organise the collection of salvage, and so decided it would be a good way to combine war-work with making new friends. To this end, I enlisted the help of a thirteen-year-old schoolboy (Stuart Garret, of no. 71 Wynn Road) who lived a few doors away. Luckily, he had a homemade barrow of the soapbox variety, which proved extremely useful as we visited the houses in our immediate neighbourhood. Happily, the people on whom we called were very responsive – and also amused – and contributed paper, rags, woollens and metal, etc. We collectors were amused too, as we must have been likened to the rag-and-bone merchants of the past. It proved to be great fun for my young assistant and we both certainly made many friends. There was even a letter of commendation from the

Jessie, with salvage collecting assistant Stuart Garret (no. 71), and neighbour Alice Almond, outside Alice's bungalow Greenwood, at the bottom end of Wynn Road.

council. [Editor's note: Joy also delighted in being pushed around Tankerton in the soapbox; that is, until space was required for the collected salvage.]

In addition to our small efforts, people had been asked to part with their iron fences for the war effort and many did just that, but that was not my department – and way beyond my physical capabilities. However, I had another idea that would help. I suggested that the local authority should open one of the derelict shops and let me see what I could do with it for the salvage scheme. They agreed, and so I set to work printing slogans on the windows. Soon, salvage was flowing in freely; so much, in fact, that I had to get others to help me. [Editor's note: the shop in question was situated at no. 137 Tankerton Road, and a picture of it – together with one of the Wynn Road salvage collection teams – is seen below. No. 137 is a cut-flower shop today, and has changed remarkably little in the intervening years.]

'Saucepans for Spitfires' was the slogan on many a wall poster, and I clearly remember parting up with my best aluminium set, riding down the street with all three saucepans dangling from the handlebars of my bicycle. During our regular salvage collection sorties, I found out that my teenage assistant, Stuart, was the son of another sailor, so I made a further friend of his mother: a friendly and happy-go-lucky Scotswoman. In fact, we struck up a very close friendship and I found that she was a real tonic to be with, especially with our mutual interest – the Royal Navy. [Editor's note: Stuart's parents were Ted (?) and Nan Garret. In fact, Stuart's father made up the third sailor of the group locally known as 'The Three Musketeers' who are mentioned elsewhere in this book. As it turned out, no. 71 Wynn Road – also called St Donatts – would later play a significant role in my family's future, more of which later.]

Salvage collection resulted in further acquaintances in the form of a dear old couple in our part of the road. The husband was an ex-sea captain who went about with a little box of peppermints in his pocket. Inevitably, he was a favourite of Joy's and never failed to produce the expected sweetie whenever they met. On the other side of our house lived two elderly ladies.

The salvage shop at no. 137 Tankerton Road.

We kept on finding more and more pairs of elderly ladies; it must have been the Whitstable air! This particular pair didn't believe in newspapers but produced some old woollens for our salvage collection.

Opposite us, I met an ex-army musical director, by the name of McBurn (spelling uncertain), who had seen better days, having conducted regimental bands all over the world in his time. He was an elderly single gentleman, and found life very hard to manage. [Editor's note: Modesty forbade my grandmother from mentioning that she regularly eased this poor man's burden by helping him with his daily chores. My grandfather would also help tend the neglected garden whenever he was home on leave. In gratitude, the old chap once gave Jessie a delightful pair of art deco Limousin figurines, and wouldn't take no for an answer. I have since been fortunate enough to have inherited them.]

Also opposite was another man by the name of Jim Crow (or Crowe). He had a bed-ridden wife, whom nobody in the road had ever seen, and the poor old chap had to do all the cooking, the nursing and shopping, as well as everything else in the home. Later on, the strain must have been a contributory cause of his death. When his niece came to see to the wife, clear up the house and also take the invalid away to live with her, they called in a specialist to overhaul the patient. To everyone's amazement, she was declared to be a fit woman – nothing that fresh air and exercise couldn't put right. Her life had been a hoax for ten years; it's hard to believe that anyone could behave like that.

Yet another elderly couple across the road became very friendly with us and were a source of great comfort to us when news was bad about shipping in the Mediterranean.

One day, I went to an auction sale in Whitstable High Street and bought a job lot for 4s, because I had taken a fancy to one particular vase, but I had to have the whole load of junk along with it. It proved intriguing when I found an old Gladstone bag at the bottom of the box, which was locked. There was no key, so I took the bag to our friend who managed to break it open. We were then to discover that the bag had a false bottom, under which what appeared to be a full bottle of whisky. I knew that my husband would not be interested as he was teetotal, so I gave it to our handy friend. He looked at it carefully, and also sniffed the contents, but he wasn't sure. However, he thought it must be alright, because the label said so. Even so, he still hesitated, and it was weeks before he plucked up courage to sample the contents, and I am pleased to report that it was the real stuff. And we had great fun imagining the secret drinker who had hidden the evidence from his wife.

There was, by this time, much talk of firebombs and firewatchers would be needed, so I joined up for our road. There was one other volunteer in our road, and we were supplied with stirrup pumps and long-handled scoops for the treatment of incendiary bombs. We were also issued with protective helmets. These were not at all comfortable, so in the cold weather, we wore scarves over them.

In our case, nothing much happened, and we had no fires to fight, but we were ready just in case. We were fortunate when so many others were suffering from this insidious menace. Whenever there was an alert, we ARP volunteers kept watch. At night, the ear-piercing noise of bombs often shattered our dreams and out I would go to join my colleague on patrol. Being young and healthy, I had no objection to walking up and down the road watching for trouble. Joy was perfectly safe, tucked up in the Morrison shelter, which had been installed in our downstairs front room. It had a solid steel tabletop and a cage-like base into which a little family could squeeze in time of need. We made a bed in it and Joy would sometimes awake during a raid, but she remained quite content so long as she had her sweet ration. And then, as we firewatchers passed the house, one or other would call into her for mutual reassurance, and she was no trouble at all.

Jessie's ARP card, issued for firewatching duties in Wynn Road and adjacent streets. Note the spelling mistake!

FP5/6.

WHITSTABLE A.R.P.

This is to Certify *that*

Mrs.Dine,

61, Wynn Road.

has enrolled and been accepted as a Fire Watcher.

(signed)

A.R.P Controller

Date   1/3/41

N.B.—This authority must be produced on request by Police or other authorised persons.   *Jessie E. Vine.*

Joy safely tucked up in bed, within the internal Morrison shelter, which was designed to survive the weight of a house falling on it.

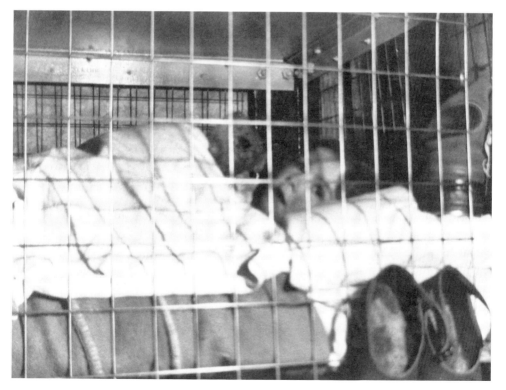

In addition to the multitude of internal Morrison and external Anderson shelters, there were also public air raid shelters throughout Whitstable, packed around with sandbags. On top of all that, every household had buckets of sand and water at the ready.

Posters were in evidence on all spare windows and walls with slogans, exhortations and many vital messages – 'Careless talk costs lives', 'Keep it under your hat' and 'Look out – there's a spy about'. One other image familiar to all was the squander bug, pointing out the errors of unnecessary spending, and the merits of war-savings. Another character that appeared everywhere – for the large part in an unofficial graffiti-like capacity – was an ugly little cartoon face depicted peeping over a wall, and he would say things such as, 'What, no meat?' It was called 'Chad', for some reason, and the words varied from time to time, according to the particular shortage that rankled the most at the time. [Editor's note: Other familiar wartime slogans included, both official and unofficial, 'Don't you know there's a war on?'; 'Put that Light out!'; 'Be like Dad, keep Mum'; 'Save petrol and use shanks's pony'; 'Is your journey really necessary?'; 'Waste not, want not'; and 'Walls have ears,' to which was often added 'but they also have good sausages'.]

CHAD

Tom's take on the 'Chad' character, which could be seen on many a Whitstable wall during the Second World War.

Another of Tom Vine's drawings, this one being the swastika-clad 'Squander Bug', pointing out the errors of needless waste.

SQUANDER BUG

14

PHOTOGRAPHY

Soon after Tom had gone to sea, I set to work thinking what I could do to put some love and interest into his life while he was away from us. I soon thought about snapshots. They are always so welcome when one is away from home but, by this time, films were almost impossible to get. And then I found that my old Kodak Brownie camera contained an unfinished film, admittedly long past its expiry date, and forgotten in the traumas of events since I had loaded the modest camera many months previously.

Undaunted, I obtained a book on developing and printing and, in the blackout of my little kitchen, I began to experiment. I'd managed to locate a red electric bulb, some developing fluid and fixer, and some very out-of-date printing paper.

Blowing a kiss to Tom: one of the many self-taken, and self-developed pictures that Jessie sent out to her husband on the HMS *Euryalus* in the Med.

Reading a bedtime story to Joy. Jessie always took great pains to conceal the light button in her hand, which enabled the exposure to take place.

A picture capturing a typical teatime at no. 61 Wynn Road, but a family scene that would have meant so much to Tom.

Sampling the homemade pickled onions: another of Tom Vine's favourites. Note the unopened jar, marked 'for Daddy'.

My first attempt at making pictures was a tolerable success and the definition wasn't too bad at all. Deciding that second-rate pictures would be better than nothing at all, I got on my bike, while Joy was at school, and visited all the chemists in the district, in search of film. I did the same thing in Faversham and succeeded in collecting a little stock of some very chancy, long out-of-date material.

I was only too willing to take the chance of getting some pictures of home that would bring happiness to Tom. Letters meant so much to the men at sea, especially as there were times when nothing arrived for anything up to six weeks.

I made holders from old wire to fit electric bulbs (strong wattage – about 200w) and got a reasonably bright light for indoor night-time pictures. In addition, I led a flex from the wall switch, with a push button at the end. Placing my box camera in a convenient position in the room, from which I could focus a pre-arranged position in the immediate vicinity, I then put the room in darkness. Next, I had to grope my way in the gloom to the chosen position (first having opened the lens) and then, with the push button hidden about my person, I flicked on the light for a few seconds and clicked it off again.

The next thing to do was feel my way back to the camera and then close the lens. Thus a self-portrait had been taken. I created quite a lot of pictures this way, showing us at no. 61 in familiar surroundings, routines and conditions that would all mean 'home' to Tom. I also photographed Joy when she was in bed asleep, when she was having a bath, sending kisses to Daddy, the two of us having a meal, me playing the piano, even doing the washing up. [Editor's note: My mother remembers that, although she was only too pleased to do something for her father, she found the many long exposures – and strict instructions about how to pose herself – a little wearing after a while, especially at mealtimes, when all she really wanted to do was tuck in.]

One particular picture was rather like a long-distance tease, and showed a 'still life' of his own personal gear: pipe-rack, hat, alarm clock, slippers, jigsaw puzzle, favourite tie, garden knife, and a tempting plate of mince pies. All my amateur photographic efforts meant that with every letter Tom received, there was always something extra to look forward to. He told me afterwards that these treasures meant so much to him that he wore them, with other personal items (money and identification, etc) in a waterproof belt, in case the worst happened at sea. A sailor never knew when he would have to jump overboard quickly. These homemade snapshots were with him all through the war. [Editor's note: A number of these self-same pictures are reproduced throughout this book. Few of the original negatives have survived, so what you see are the actual prints that my grandfather valued so dearly.]

15

UNITED IN TROUBLE

Ｍy parents (Charles and Caroline Tomlin) were in Dover, as were Tom's widowed mother (Emily Vine) and other relations (including Emily's half-sister, and constant companion, Mary Ann Johnson, or 'Aunt Polly'). The town was taking a lot of punishment, constantly being shelled from across the Channel. The Germans had mounted long-range guns on the coast between Calais and Boulogne, and the shelling became a daily occurrence, until 'Hell-Fire Corner' became a very apt name. After bombing shipping in the Channel, the enemy did their best to annihilate the important port of Dover, along with the town, and many people had to leave family surroundings for safer areas. [Editor's note: As

Jessie's parents, Charles and Carrie Tomlin, during a Christmas family gathering at Three Bridges in Sussex, 1941.

Tom and Ivy's mother, Emily Vine, outside her Dover home, no. 17 East Cliff, which she shared with her half-sister, Mary Ann Johnson, better known as 'Aunt Polly'.

a child, Jessie had personally experienced bombing in Dover, from Zeppelins in the First World War, as vividly described in the first volume of her memoirs, *Dover Remembered*.]

To escape the shelling, my mother went to Crawley in Sussex, leaving Dad behind because of his work, at least in the short-term. She was welcomed by loving hands, for my youngest sister Grace had already set up home there, after she and her fiancé (Reg Grime), a precision engineer on important war work, had decided to marry earlier than planned and move to his new place of work. The war caused so many plans to be changed and many people found themselves in totally unexpected places where, so often, they put down roots and stayed. [Editor's note: Jessie's sister-in-law and fellow Rochester evacuee, Ivy Hookham, had also decided to settle in Tankerton, having acquired no. 15 Ellis Road, as mentioned in an earlier chapter. In this house, they were soon joined by Gran Vine (Tom and Ivy's mother) and Aunt Polly, hitherto of East Cliff, Dover, both of whom were desperate to escape the shelling of the town. And as conditions got even worse, several other relations abandoned Dover for temporary shelter elsewhere.]

The shelling of Dover was very heavy and, inevitably, we heard that my parents' home in Effingham Crescent had been badly damaged like so many others. The local authorities had done their best to cope with the amount of work entailed in boarding up unoccupied premises, but with the available work force, it was impossible to get them all done before wind and weather took thier toll. During a quiet spell, my mother and I planned to meet at the house in order to sort a few belongings, to see the extent of the damage and to retrieve whatever we could. On the journey down to Dover, it came home forcibly to me that Kent was indeed the front-line county.

Upon reaching our destination, we found a sight that I'll never forget. During the time that the place had been open to the weather, the rain and dampness had taken their toll, and we left footsteps in the mildew wherever we walked. Sadly though, apart from enemy action, the place had also been ransacked from end-to-end, and looted very thoroughly. Every drawer and cupboard had been opened and the contents emptied onto the floors, which were littered with debris that had once been valued family belongings. Much had been stolen and my mother and I felt like weeping. However, we rallied and then looked around for a while in search of a few remaining personal things to take home with us. It was then that we had the nastiest shock of all: to find human excreta on the dining room floor. It was like a hammer blow to our hearts and the very last straw; we just couldn't bear any more. I will draw a veil over this calamity, but suffice to say, my mother never returned to the old family home.

'Aunt Polly', in the back garden of no. 15 Ellis Road, Tankerton, shortly after she and Emily Vine had been relocated from Dover.

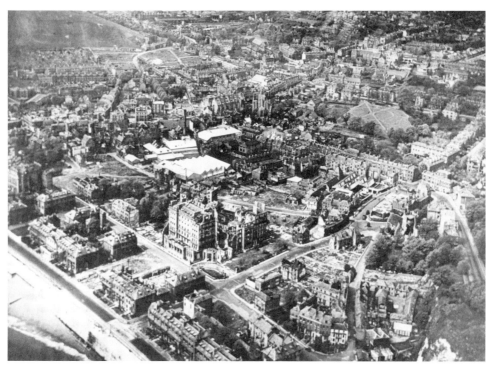

Dover in the aftermath of war. An aerial picture, from 1946, clearly showing the damage caused to the town by constant shelling from occupied Europe. *(Photograph courtesy of Topix/Thomson Newspapers Ltd)*

Tom's drawing of the 'old' St James' Church in Dover: the Tomlin family's place of worship until 1940. The church was badly damaged by shell fire and the tower collapsed in the early post-war period.

I returned to Whitstable, after seeing my mother off to Crawley, carrying a few odds-and-ends, which I would find useful while commodities were unobtainable. I also took with me tragic memories of the loss of familiar landmarks and buildings in my hometown of Dover. I especially grieved at the severe damage caused to the 'old' St James' Church, which had meant so much to me in childhood. This now stands as a 'tidy ruin'; a grim reminder of the futility of war.

I REMEMBER by Jessie
The churches that we loved so well
Since childhood's pleasant days,
When kindly parsons led our feet
Thro' straight and narrow ways.

These ancient consecrated stones
Were raised above the clod,
By loving hands of humble men
To glorify their God.

These lovely hallowed buildings
Where yew trees guard the door,
And quaint old lichgates, where the dead
Passed through to toil no more.

The birdsong from the cedars
Blends with the organ swells,
And from the tower high above
The peal of friendly bells.

When we were young, each Sunday morn
We went in groups to pray,
To thank God for his blessings
And sanctify His day.

We watched the fond young parents
Bring infants to be blest,
Where stained glass windows showed the Lord
With lambs held to his breast.

At Eastertide, we gathered flowers,
To dress each aisle and pew,
And sang the hymn of risen Christ
And hope was born anew.

And when the summer days were passed
And crops were gathered in,
We raised with grateful hearts and souls
Each joyful harvest hymn.

Then winter came and Christmas-tide
And carols we would sing,
Of shepherds and the newborn babe
Who was the saviour King.

Where is the calm of yesteryear?
The peace for which we search?
Tranquillity and rest are found
Inside an ancient church.

16

SHARING THE ORANGES

One day, a group of us went for a walk across the fields with two aims in mind: to buy some windfall apples from the orchard that was owned by a very nice lady, and to see if there were any remains of a downed Messerschmitt we'd heard about. [Editor's note: This walk took them south from Tankerton, and then along the, as yet, largely undeveloped Clover Rise.]

There were seven of us, comprising four children, the minister, his wife and myself. The minister – the Revd Mr Williams, already mentioned in previous chapters – was a well-set-up man of about thirty-four, very active and well loved by his largely elderly congregation. His wife took part in all the work of the church, which was a fairly new, red-brick building in Northwood Road, very unlike the ancient churches that I had always attended in both Dover and Rochester.

We were all enjoying the country walk in the lovely early autumn sunshine, that is, until we had to shelter under a hedge while another dogfight was in progress in the skies directly above us. When the engagement was over, we continued on our way, with our dual quest still very much in mind. Sadly, it soon became clear that the crashed enemy plane we sought had been quickly cleared away, and no trace of it remained. [Editor's note: There is a well-documented account of a Spitfire crash at Rayham Road, at the south end of Clover Rise, but I cannot as yet confirm that a Messerschmitt came down in this vicinity.]

After we had stopped for a short while, the minister's wife, to our surprise, produced two oranges from her pocket and handed them to her husband. We all watched in awe as he peeled them very carefully, and then, having separated the segments, he took off his hat, blessed the fruit and then shared it between the seven of us. It was very generous of them to share their precious oranges, so hard to get hold of as we knew them to be. However, I couldn't help (irreverently perhaps) likening this episode to the miracle of the loaves and fishes in the Bible, especially as I remembered, 'and they took up the fragments', for Mrs Williams carefully retained all the peel to take home with which to make some wartime-style marmalade, mixed with the windfall apples we also hoped to obtain that day. [Editor's note: My mother remembers that, on the way home, there was either an air raid warning, or another dogfight, which caused the party to run for home, rather than shelter under a hedge as before. In crossing the 'Thanet Way' arterial road, my grandmother had a nasty fall, and cut her leg rather badly.]

One weekend, I took Joy to a cinema in Whitstable to see two very special films: the immensely popular *Mrs Miniver*; a very touching story, and Noel Coward's story of life in a destroyer at sea called *In Which We Serve*. It is very understandable why I wanted to see the latter-named film in particular. It was faithful in its detail and had great appeal to all patriotic people. In fact, both

Early 'Battle of Britain' vapour trails in the skies above Whitstable as another dogfight takes place. *(Douglas West Collection, Whitstable Museum and Gallery copyright)*

'Look pleasant please!' Bob and Ivy Hookham, with Ivy's brother Ted Vine (a policeman up from Dover), in the back garden of no. 15 Ellis Road, Tankerton, at about the time of the Battle of Britain.

All Saints' Church, Whitstable – taken between the wars – to which Jessie and Joy went after 'the snub'.

of these pictures affected me deeply, as my heart was already full to overflowing with sorrow and misgivings, wondering where my husband was. If ever a film pulled at the heartstrings and set-flow the tears, then this one did just that to me, and to a good many others besides, especially the Navy wives.

The next time we bumped in to each other, I innocently mentioned to the minister's wife that I had been to the cinema to see these films. Consequently, the next day at the Sunday Service, I was more than surprised while listening to the theme of the minister's sermon. The front row was taken up by Boy Scouts, and they were told, 'don't go to the cinema boys; they're dirty; they're corrupt!' I just couldn't believe my ears and felt very strongly that this was all being directed at me. If he and I had made eye contact during this apocalyptic warning, then I may have had my worst fears confirmed! It was probably my state of mind that made me feel this way: having such a worrying time and being full of anxieties, with tears never very far away in those dark days.

After that snub – which I felt it was – I moved to the church where I felt I really belonged: All Saints', in Church Road, which is Church of England. It wasn't far away, and was such a lovely building, with elements dating back to the thirteenth century (many years later, my daughter Joy would get married there).

Church bells had been silenced for the duration, so we had no welcoming peal of bells on a Sunday morning for a long time. Whenever that poignant hymn, written by William Whiting, is sung, it takes me straight back to those war years:

> Eternal Father strong to save,
> Whose arm doth guide the restless wave,
> Who bids the mighty ocean deep,
> its own appointed limits keep.
> O hear us when we cry to Thee,
> For those in peril on the sea.

That hymn always has, and always will be profoundly moving to seafarers and their families.

17

THE BOMBING ESCALATES

By 14 June 1940 we heard, with great sadness, that Paris had fallen to the Germans. Our hearts went out to the French people, who had resisted so valiantly. Hostilities had ceased there by the 25th and they had to live a gruelling life under the Nazi heel. By 1 July, the enemy had occupied the Channel Islands. It was all getting too near for comfort, but soon Britain had to take a very real testing, for the Battle of Britain began on 10 July, with a vengeance unknown to most of us before. This historic happening has been recorded frequently and the sad tales of sorrow, suffering and courage never fails to move us to the depths. [Editor's note: the dramatic sights of dogfights, with their arcing vapour trails, were an almost daily occurrence in the skies over Whitstable during this period.]

A badly damaged bungalow in St Swithin's Road, Tankerton, on 28 August 1940. (*Douglas West Collection, Whitstable Museum and Gallery copyright*)

A devastated house at Bartlett's Corner, between Church Street, Whitstable and Ham Shades Lane, Tankerton, on 5 October 1941. The junction for Bridewell Park occupies the site today. *(Douglas West Collection, Whitstable Museum and Gallery copyright)*

A chimney stack is all that has been left standing of this once impressive, detached house in Ham Shades Lane, Tankerton. The date is 5 October 1941. *(Douglas West Collection, Whitstable Museum and Gallery copyright)*

A bomb in the road ripped up all the mains services at the top end of Pier Avenue on 20 October 1940. Shops on the south side of Tankerton Road can be seen in the background. *(Douglas West Collection, Whitstable Museum and Gallery copyright)*

The same stick of bombs on 20 October 1940 made a crater in the middle of Graystone Road, just south of its junction with Tankerton Road. *(Douglas West Collection, Whitstable Museum and Gallery copyright).*

No sooner had the Battle of Britain been substantially won, then the Blitz of London began in earnest. The bravery of the men and women of our capital city was beyond belief. People really suffered, relentlessly night after night, when bombs and incendiaries lit up the London sky turning night into day. [Editor's note: The London Blitz is widely documented as beginning on 7 September 1940. As the dramatic pictures from the Douglas West Archive make clear – six of which are reproduced in this book – Whitstable and Tankerton suffered considerably during the early weeks of the London Blitz, and the overlapping tail-end of the Battle of Britain period, especially on 28 September, and 5, 11, and 20 October 1940.]

In the newspapers and on the newsreels, we could all witness that King George VI and his lovely Queen Elizabeth were frequently to be seen among the wreckage of the London streets, sympathising, encouraging and cheering the hapless victims of the Blitz. Their indomitable resolution and spirit stirred the world, and the Britain people really showed that 'we can take it'.

I cannot properly describe the devastation in London, for I was not there. Only those who had to bear it can tell of the full horror. However, I know very well – from the relatively small bombing in our immediate vicinity – that it must have been hell let loose, and the world will always admire the endurance and bravery of those who went through those endless days and nights of torture.

Canterbury under fire; Barretts in St Peter's Street goes up in flames. Such blazes, caused by incendiary bombs, could be seen from miles away, including in Whitstable and Tankerton. *(Fisk Moore Collection)*

On 14 November 1940, Coventry was attacked in much the same manner, but with short and severe ferocity, followed by the very heavy bombing of Bristol. As far as bombing raids were concerned, 1941 was a relatively quiet year, especially in our part of East Kent. However, the following year would be very different. By far the worst attack of 1942, near us, was the Baedeker raid on the city of Canterbury, so called because of the guidebook of that name, which listed towns and cities of special historical interest.

It was the early hours of 31 May into 1 June 1942, and when it was all happening, we in Whitstable could clearly hear the appalling explosions, as the world itself seemed to be tearing apart. It had started quietly, with the slowly dropping flares that lit up the night sky. Then came the numerous incendiaries, but it was the screaming of high-explosive bombs, mixed with the frightening roar of engines, which awakened us all on the coast, some 7 miles away. It was then that the realisation hit home that the much-loved old city was getting one of the worst raids to date.

I had been on ARP duty in Wynn Road that night and was still in uniform when the raid began. I was soon joined by many of my neighbours, in their nightclothes, and we all stood there in the street, looking southwards in sheer disbelief at the sight. And as we stared in amazement at the unholy red-orange glow that hung over the city, it appeared to be engulfing the entire area, and we wept for the people of Canterbury. Opinion was unanimous that no one could have survived such an onslaught; the people of the cathedral city must surely have been wiped out. There couldn't be anyone or anything left, we all sadly concluded; it looked so very awful. There were also great palls of smoke and columns of flame, as streets and lanes, as well as houses both large and small all went up with a roar. Yes, we could also hear the Blitz of Canterbury and, before very long, the acrid smell of the burning city even drifted over to us.

Finally, we all slowly and sadly retuned to our beds, grieving for the losses of people and places so familiar to us all, and so important to our national heritage. However, when we had

One of the only known pictures of Judy, with 'Gran' and Bob Hookham, in the front garden of no. 15 Ellis Road, Tankerton.

St George's Street, Canterbury's main shopping thoroughfare, in the immediate aftermath of the 1 June 1942 Blitz. Note the upstanding tower of St George's Church, which survives to this day. *(Fisk Moore Collection)*

the opportunity to go and see the devastation for ourselves, we were astonished to see the beloved cathedral standing there in most of its glory, towering above the surrounding chaos liken a sign from God.

The rebuilding of Canterbury would be some years away but, in the meantime, its local people took stock of the situation and work began immediately, clearing the whole area of rubble and restoring some sort of life back into the city centre once more. Reflections of the British character shone out like a beacon light in the Stygian gloom of that Monday morning in early June, and we can admire the stoicism of the venerable old Canterbury gentleman, out in the dust-laden air, picking his way over still-smoking ruins on a mercy mission who, upon meeting a lady of his acquaintance, still remembered to raise his hat.

After the horrors of that never-to-be-forgotten night of the infamous Baedeker raid, there were many sad incidents among the pets of Canterbury. Birds escaped from their cages and flew away to chance their luck among the indigenous birds of the air. Two budgerigars found their way to Tankerton and defied all efforts to catch them.

Cats and dogs also suffered and were made homeless like their owners and, terrified, they cowered in corners, too shocked to move or, otherwise, ran and ran until exhaustion finally overcame them. One such pitiful story concerned a small dog called Judy, who was found shivering badly and quietly howling outside 'Gran's' house (Emily Vine) at no. 15 Ellis Road, Tankerton. Having only recently escaped the shelling of Dover, Tom's mum knew what it was to hasten away from enemy terrors and, taking pity on the sad little mongrel, she took it in and tenderly calmed it – giving it warm milk and a comfortable bed. [Editor's note: My mother's cousin, Bob Hookham, recalls the incident slightly differently, and thinks that Judy first arrived at the house of Alice Almond – a Hookham relative – at Greenwood in Wynn Road, but that the little dog was then quickly adopted by 'Gran Vine', who bonded with her immediately.]

The unfortunate creature had a name and address on its collar, which made it obvious that she had travelled all night the 7 miles distance from the horrors of the Canterbury Blitz to the relative calm of a leafy Whitstable suburb. Her coat was matted and dirty and there was broken glass in her paws. She smelled rather badly as if she had waded through all sorts of muck, so she wasn't a pretty sight at all, but the look in her eyes said it all.

Subsequent enquiries revealed that Judy's original owner's house had been devastated and the occupants had 'gone away'. Therefore, she became an orphan of war and the very much-loved pet of an old lady, who cherished her little companion until the end of her days. [Editor's note: During the main raid – 1 June 1942 – on Canterbury, a high-explosive bomb had ruptured a mains sewer pipe at the junction of Beer Cart Lane with Stour Street, and some of the people living nearby, who had been sheltering in their cellars, had tragically drowned in effluent. This could very well be an explanation of Judy's state, and possibly also her origin.]

After those first few days of June 1942, it was obvious that, for us at least, it had all really started. And yet, we on the coast had not had to experience anything too terrible, other than

The devastation in Beer Cart Lane, Canterbury: the likely place that the stray dog Judy had fled from, before journeying all the way to Tankerton. *(Photograph courtesy of RCHM)*

Joy with her pet cat Ginger, which she used to dress-up in doll's clothes.

the occasional ditching of bombs by German airmen in a great hurry to get home, and lighten their deadly load on the way. On one such occasion, when a stick of bombs was jettisoned near to us, all seven were dropped into the sea, near the shoreline, and did nobody any harm. However, the scars were visible over a long period of time, with each receding tide exposing great heaps of disturbed sand.

Another Messerschmitt came down a short distance away from us in the fields, and the pilot parachuted to earth and gave himself up with no trouble whatsoever. Those who saw his descent said that he made no effort to escape but went quietly, probably only too pleased to be out of it all for the duration. Local witnesses also said that he was little more than a boy: somebody's son. Now though, his war was over. [Editor's note: This incident may be related to the downed plane mentioned in the previous chapter.]

When another particular alert had sounded, Joy was busily dressing her protesting kitten (Ginger) in dolly clothes. Despite the hisses and scratches, Joy persisted until she had fastened a bonnet on its head with a huge blue bow under the chin. Then she struggled with a long gown, which covered both hind legs and tail. Tied round the middle with another bow and with two little paws poking through the armholes, Ginger finally escaped, just as the siren was sounding. On this occasion, the gunfire started almost immediately afterwards, and the poor frightened little creature shot out of the house, down the garden path, and then went straight up the clothes pole to the very top.

Poor Ginger stayed there for the best part of two hours with the bonnet at a drunken angle, clinging on for dear life, and no amount of cajoling or calling would entice it to come down. It seemed to prefer the sound of enemy gunfire to the ministrations of its little mistress. There we were in the relative safety of the house, and all we could do was worry about the safety of that small oddly dressed pussy.

18

AS TIME GOES BY

Life had to continue; we all had to do the best we could with available resources. Many of us made a habit of listening to the Kitchen Front radio and heard that folk were better off if they had allotments. Consequently, I decided to do something about it and asked if I could use a spare plot of land at the end of the road as an allotment. Having obtained permission, I had the gigantic task of digging it and this I managed to do bit by bit. [Editor's not: The allotment was on a vacant plot in Wynn Road, near the Northwood Road junction. There is a house occupying the site today.]

My little girl helped with the weeds on our formative allotment. I used bribery and corruption, of course, as most children need a little coaxing when there's work to be done. Best of all, I promised her a 'putty medal' at the end of the war. This eventually took the shape of a huge doll, which I bought as soon as they were available. [Editor's note: The doll, lovingly named Judy – the same as Gran's stray dog – was actually purchased from Barrett's in St Peter's Street, Canterbury. This must have been at some time shortly before 22 January 1944, as a single incendiary bomb destroyed their entire premises in the early hours of that day.]

Joy also acquired two little bantams as pets, supposedly too old to lay, but surprise-surprise, they began to produce a few eggs, which were very acceptable, small as they were. These we kept in our back garden for safety. We added a couple of brown pullets to these and took a great interest in watching for precious eggs, and were very dismayed when we discovered the presence of rats.

Something had to be done, and quickly. So I set a trap for several days, but that rat was a very cunning creature and defeated me. He may have won the first round, but I didn't like losing to a rat. Drastic measures were clearly called for. I found Tom's Webly Scott air pistol and tried a few practise shots. I then sat on the roof of the garden shed, sighting the weapon on the rat-hole. There I sat, rigidly still for one and a half hours until I ached all over. And then, a nose and whiskers slowly appeared, and out he came, taking the bait I'd laid and slow dragging it back to the hole. It was then that I let go with the pistol and he promptly disappeared. I thought I was thwarted once more. The next week, I set traps once again and finally caught a rat with a crippled leg, so I'd got my little chicken food robber at last.

Food for this small group of hens was hard to come by, and even potato peelings were a prized asset. On top of that, spasmodic raids continued – and more items came on to the ration list. A points system had come into force during December 1941, as everything was in such short supply. In the following year, soap was also rationed, much to the delight of small boys!

Joy outside the hospital hut in Pier Avenue, Tankerton. The hut is still there today, although direct access from Pier Avenue is no longer possible.

Joy on her bicycle outside no. 61 Wynn Road, Tankerton.

Joy gets in on the act and proudly wears the bridesmaid's dress, also made from available wartime materials by Jessie.

Jessie poses in the wedding dress she made for the next-door neighbours' daughter, Joan Taylor.

Utility clothes were the mode, but they didn't interest me, for I found it more individual to get material and make our own garments. Make-do and mend was the patriotic thing to do and many people took pride in adapting new garments from old ones: even turning coats inside out and remaking them to the un-faded side.

Most people had a fear of possible parachutists. Rumours had reached us that enemy spies were descending from the skies dressed as nuns! To be honest, I was much more interested in getting hold of the parachute material, like so many other wives, for we found we could make such a lot with it and save on the clothing coupons. Indeed, from this highly valued material, could be made knickers, petticoats blouses, etc. [Editor's notes: Jessie's dressmaking skills soon became a talking point at their end of Wynn Road and, as a result, she was asked to make the wedding dress and bridesmaid's outfits for the next-door neighbours' daughter, Joan Taylor at no. 59.]

As time went on and there were no evacuees to occupy my daylight hours, I had to fill my time, because any inactivity meant dwelling on the grim possibilities of what might happen. One had to have faith, but to fill one's mind made it necessary to be very busy, with no time to sit and think. By now, Joy was seven years old and was attending a private school for the sole reason that it was near to home and that meant less worry. [Editor's note: This was the Parents' National Educational Union School – or P.N.E.U. – in Gloucester Road. It was run by the highly regarded Margaret Proctor.]

Like most schools, they were short of staff due to war conditions and I filled a gap by helping out, although I was not a qualified teacher. I liked the work and got on with the children and staff very nicely, and as my efforts were found to be acceptable, all went well. The arrangement proved very satisfactory for me, for when the raids took place, I was under the same roof as my child. I also found that I had an aptitude for this kind of work and I enjoyed taking books home to mark during evenings, as well as making preparations for the coming day.

The original inscription on the back of this snap read, 'April 15th 1942: Joy, the big school girl – full of dinner – just going back to school!' However, she doesn't look too happy at the prospect!

Miss Proctor, principal of the P.N.E.U. School, enjoys a game with some of her pupils. Joy is to her right, and eating as usual!

Joy Vine and her best friend, Sylvia White, in the uniforms of the P.N.E.U. School, in Gloucester Road, Whitstable.

Some of the pupils and teachers of the P.N.E.U. School, on an outing, near the Thanet Way. Note the Canterbury to Whitstable Railway bridge in the background (Jessie is on the far left).

Haw-Haw's threats and sneers continued throughout this period and I tried not to listen to the broadcasts, but still heard all about it from other people. So the anxieties went on. Thousands of people were losing sleep just like me, hoping for the best, yet fearing for the worst. Heartbreaking losses, both Naval and mercantile, made us all fearful of what we might hear next. HMS *Barham* was sunk, another shocking blow to the nation, and then the Japanese attack on Pearl Harbor made a colossal mark in world history that will never be forgotten, but close to our hearts came another great loss. We heard, with great sorrow, that HMS *Repulse* and HMS *Prince of Wales* were sunk off Malta by the same fanatical enemy.

[Editor's note: there was one key family event from this period that my grandmother omitted, for whatever reason, but for the sake of completeness, I will add it here. On 26 October 1942, Jessie and Joy moved a little way down Wynn Road, from the house at no. 61 to a bungalow at no. 71, on the same side of the street. My mother remembers it well as it was her seventh birthday. The bungalow had previously been occupied by the Garret family – mentioned elsewhere in this book – who are thought to have moved north.]

19

THOUGHTS OF THE NAVY

W e were most interested, and encouraged, to hear that the little island of Malta had been awarded the George Cross. I knew that Tom was on convoy work somewhere in the Mediterranean. However, that was far too stressful to dwell upon. Instead, I found it comforting to think of life on board a Naval ship as it was before the war. I especially remember the day we went on board the newly built HMS *Euryalus* at Chatham and had tea in the Petty Officer's mess. Sailors love little children and the men made a great fuss of Joy, who thoroughly enjoyed the adoration.

The Navy man's jargon is most amusing and all Navy wives are accustomed to it and understand the strange expressions, most of which must sound like gobbledegook to folk in Civvy Street. Some of these sayings must have had their origins in antiquity and are unique to the British Navy, especially lower deck:

'Sharp about the bows' means a man has had a new haircut
'Choc-a-bloc' means fed-up
'Up the line' means far away in thoughts; not paying attention
'Heads' means lavatories
'Deck head' means the ceiling
'Bulk head' means the wall
'Spliced' means married, and there's many more . . .

[Editor's note: One word that I remember my grandfather using all the time was 'Cungies' – I'm not sure of the spelling – which meant any sort of scented soap. As far as he was concerned, only coal-tar soap would do.]

Many lower-deck men ran so-called firms (with the captain's permission) and the most generally patronised of these was the Dhobi-Wallah: the man who did laundry. Most married men were quite happy to do their own washing, but young bachelors were often only too pleased to get this chore done for them.

There were photographic firms – very lucrative when on a foreign commission – and the drinks firm made a good thing of it in the hot climates. There were also the so-called 'Jewing' firms, making and mending; even running up a complete square rig on the old sewing machine.

There were, of course, barbers who were always busy on short-back-and-sides. However, if a man wished to grow a full set of whiskers and beard, he had to obtain permission from the captain and, by the same token, permission to shave it off.

A fine study of Chief Petty Officer Tom Vine, aboard HMS *Euryalus*, while it was docked at Alexandria in 1942.

Tom spent his spare time with gymnastics and water polo (especially in the immediate pre-war years) but in quieter moments, he took up his beloved sketching. Many men enjoyed their rum ration, but a teetotaller could have the threepence-a-day added to his pay. [Editor's note: My Grandfather had been brought up in a Wesleyan Methodist household, so strong drink never formed part of his culture, and on the few occasions he had been compelled by friends to try it, he would claim that it tasted like varnish.]

20

HOMECOMING

The British people were very glad when the Americans decided to come into the war with the Allies – the endeavour to finish off the war in Europe while hostilities in the Pacific were still being waged. They, the Americans, made a big impact on many members of our society, particularly those who lived near to bases where the 'Yanks' were stationed. They were very generous to children, giving parties for them at the camp, when more than the usual rations were enjoyed. Our American friends clearly had much more of everything and the situation was like bees to a honey pot. Of course, our new allies were naturally attracted to the ladies, who were delighted to find that nylons, chocolates and cigarettes were freely available.

We all had cause to be grateful to the Americans when they joined in with the bombing of Germany, often during daylight hours, and did their part valiantly in fighting the war against the evil of Nazism. They made their first attack on Germany in January 1943 and later in March, the RAF breached the dams of the Ruhr, in the famous Dambusters Raid. Tripoli was occupied by the English Army and British and Americans landed in Naples. Oh yes, it was all hotting up!

Our great leader continued to boost morale in Britain. Winston Churchill's immortal words have already gone down in history and the world will never forget them. Day by day, night by night, various incidents continued to stir our lives, but our experiences in Whitstable had no comparison at all to the very real hardships endured by so many ordinary people in other parts of the land. Indeed, our home life went on pretty much as usual; we carried out routine tasks, taking each day as it came.

On one particular autumn morning in 1943, I stood at the kitchen sink, washing up the few breakfast things, while gazing out of the window at the large garden of the bungalow we'd occupied for nearly a year so far. I thought of winter's fast approach and wondered if it would be a severe one, for the heavy crop of berries in the hedgerows predicted that it would be so. Yes, it was time to look out the winter woollies, shake out the blankets and get ready for shorter, colder days. We must not be caught napping when the first frost arrived, I thought, for fuel would be scarce again, and economy would be the watchword.

A familiar noise shook me from my musings. Ah, here comes the milk lady! Sure enough, her cheerful face soon appeared by my back door and I took half a pint from chilly fingers. She was another sailor's wife, working to keep her husband's job open for him, for he had joined up as 'hostilities only'. Every time she called, we chatted about our men, for we had a lot in common. I often wondered how she managed to keep going, as she was only a little woman and those milk crates are heavy. Nevertheless, she stuck to the job, always had time to chat, and I very much admired her pluck.

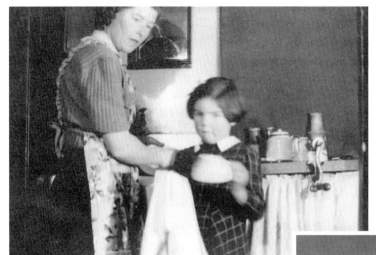

The day-to-day routine of washing up, captured for a snap to send out to Tom in the Mediterranean, where such a homely scene would mean so much.

A thinner and more introspective Tom Vine, following his gruelling tour of duty protecting the Malta Convoys.

While we chatted I heard some more footsteps and, thinking that they were on next-door's path, I took no notice. However, from where the milk-lady stood, she could see the owner of those footsteps, and I suddenly saw her face light up into a huge grin. Nothing occurred to me other than thinking that she was a cheerful little soul with a smile for everybody. And then, round the corner came Tom, totally unexpected, suitcase in hand and a smile that I'll never forget.

For a moment, I stood there in disbelief, and then I was being crushed almost to breathlessness by warm, familiar arms.

'Thank God, thank God you're safe!' I said, through barely controlled tears.

After the initial emotional greeting was over, I looked at him again, and could scarcely believe my eyes, for he appeared so different. Here was a Tom that I'd never seen before. He had always been a picture of rip-roaring health, with muscles that had been developed over the many years of Naval sports activities. However, build-wise, this man before me now could almost have been a stranger. His cheekbones were showing through and there was an odd look about his eyes, which were gaunt and hollow. It soon became clear that he was also finding hearing difficult, and this condition remained for quite some time afterwards, for over two years of heavy gunfire had taken its toll.

Later on, during that first wonderful homecoming day, when Joy came home from school, she stood there staring at first, almost frozen to the spot. The period of Tom's absence at sea had been a long time in a child's life; she had to endure over two years without a father. Soon though, there was that old familiar ritual of a leap and a hug, and the years melted away in an instant. It was wonderful to see.

Joy with some of the doll's house furniture that had been made aboard HMS *Euryalus*, in between engagements.

With his beloved daughter home, Tom began to unpack his case, and out came seven little pieces of wooden furniture for a doll's house. He soon told us how he'd started one day, whittling away with a penknife in the Petty Officer's mess, when one fellow said, 'What are you trying to make? C'mon, give it here!'

Tom's colleague then had a good go at making the first piece of furniture; after all, he was a chippy (carpenter) and knew what he was doing, while Tom was a gunnery man. Very soon, another man stepped in and also had a go, and before long the whole mess contributed to the making of a present for a lucky little girl. [Editor's note: As it turned out, many of my grandfather's colleagues had remembered Joy from the family visit day back at Chatham in the spring of 1941, just before the *Euryalus* had set sail for the first time, and were only too happy to participate.]

The doll's house furniture set was beautifully made: sofa, chairs, bed and dressing table, all made from odds and ends from all around the ship. The tiny mirror in the dressing table was a piece from a gun-sight and the whole effect was quite a work of art. The job had actually provided a welcome diversion for the men when the ship had been in dock at Alexandria. The little set has been treasured all these years, for it went through all those gruelling months of convoy protection work in the Mediterranean.

With regards to my husband's uncharacteristic thinness, I knew immediately that something had to be done about this; I must build him back up again in the best way I could, war restrictions allowing. As it happened, the news soon got up and down the road that Mr Vine was home again, and kindly neighbours brought small offerings to try and help out in fattening him up a bit: half-a-pound of sugar here, a quarter of margarine there, and even a bit of cheese. Oh, I'll never forget the kindness of all those Tankerton neighbours; by their selfless donations, they tried to show me how glad they were to see him back home again safely.

Fortunately, I was also growing my own produce, not only in the gardens at no. 71, but also on the new allotment nearby. Luckily, I even had a ready source of fertiliser for my fruit and veg, in the form of a large, elderly carthorse nicknamed 'Smelly-Nellie'. She, or probably he – in spite of the nickname – hauled the coal merchant's wagon. There was never a regular delivery of coal; you got some whenever supplies could be dropped off at Whitstable Harbour, so the appearance of Smelly-Nellie, and her equally elderly charge, was always unexpected. The horse and cart always stopped outside no. 71, as we had a lamppost adjacent to our property and the horse was always tethered to it. This was also the time when Nellie would get her nosebag, and could happily munch away for a time. Joy would always swing on the gate and watch the whole unloading ritual, but she also couldn't resist going out to stroke the horse, who was very gentle animal, despite its furry fetlocks and massive size – not to mention that sweaty smell, which probably earned him/her the nickname in the first place. Inevitably, with the horse stationary for a while, and also having its dinner, there would be the usual by-product left behind on the street surface. I could see other curtains twitching opposite, and knew that my neighbours were as keen as I was to go out and gather the droppings, for their own 'Dig for Victory' efforts. Luckily though, I had the advantage of being the nearest, and was always able to be at the ready with my bucket and spade as soon as the coal merchant finally moved on to other customers.

Tom at home, in the back garden of no. 71 Wynn Road, surrounded by the produce that would help fatten him up again.

And so, I did the best I could with the available rations – as well as my home-grown produce – while Tom was on this much-needed leave, and gradually saw him building up again, and putting some flesh back on those bones. Malta, as everybody knows, had been starving, and the ship's crew were on very short rations also, and added to the non-stop strain for such a long time, it was no wonder he looked as he did.

Luckily though, Tom picked up rapidly. I also tried to make him talk about the past two years, but it was a very long time before he would open up on the subject that he clearly wanted to forget. [Editor's note: My grandfather's wartime 'adventures' aboard HMS *Euryalus* are actually documented, as an appendix, at the end of this book, together with some dramatic photographs taken during various engagements with enemy aircraft and shipping. However, there are two personal recollections not included in the appendix, and these are among the first things he confided to his wife, once he was ready to talk about his experiences in the Mediterranean.]

The first was a selfless act that Tom carried out on more than one occasion, when the *Euryalus* was under fire. While overseeing the firing of some of the heavy guns, he had to order men to go down into the magazine and load the much-needed munitions, which would then be automatically lifted to the gunnery position above. Younger ratings often begged him not to be sent down to the magazine – pleading that they had a wife and children – knowing that if the ship were hit by returning fire, then the magazine would be the most dangerous place on the ship. And so, rather than force that particular man to carry out his order, or otherwise discipline him, my grandfather would go down himself, and continue to give his orders from below, while loading the munitions – which were constantly needed – onto the lifting mechanism. And remember, he had a wife and child too!

The other memory was a chilling eyewitness account of a Royal Navy aircraft carrier, on convoy work alongside the *Euryalus*, being hit by a torpedo, and then listing heavily before eventually sinking. The nightmare image of men sliding off the ever more sloping deck was something that stayed with him forever. The ship could have been either the HMS *Ark Royal* (which was hit on 13 November 1941, listed heavily, but sank the next day) or the HMS *Eagle*, which was hit on 11 August 1942, and also listed heavily before sinking within minutes. Neither of these dates figure in the HMS *Euryalus* diary, in the appendix – and the picture,

A nightmare that stayed with Tom for the rest of his life: the chilling sight of a Royal Naval aircraft carrier being hit by an enemy torpedo before rapidly sinking, with much loss of life.

reproduced here is very unclear – so the identity of the carrier involved will probably remain a mystery. [Editor's note: My grandmother also recalled – although she didn't include it in her memoirs – that for months after his return from the Mediterranean, he would have terrible nightmares, and often woke her up suddenly by shouting 'FIRE!' in his sleep, as he dreamt of giving gunnery orders during a nasty engagement.]

While Tom had been away, the greatest comfort was the arrival of mail. Having said that, regularly written letters often came in groups of two, or three, but they were all read over and over again, for we knew from experience that there would often be no more mail for some weeks. Tom said that another thing that did so much for the morale of the ship's company was the wonderful voice of Vera Lynn coming over the tannoy, and many a tough sailor had to pretend that he'd got grit in his eye. The favourites were 'We'll Meet Again', 'Yours till the Stars Lose Their Glory' and, of course, 'White Cliffs of Dover'. But it was something more than just a voice and a song to those men; it was a beam of light, a ray of hope and a dream of love, with all the comforts of home.

One day, a black-and-white cat, bow-legged, hump-backed and cross-eyed, came up the gangway of HMS *Euryalus* at Alexandria and made up its mind to stay on board. After obtaining the captain's permission, the cat was cleaned up and taken to the ship's doctor for neutering. He duly performed the operation and handing back the poor moggie, said, 'I hope I've taken out the right bits!' The adopted Egyptian cat was groggy for a few days, but very soon picked up and was soon christened, for obvious reasons, 'Minus'. He soon became a well-loved part of the crew, and quickly found his way to the galley. He also got to know the bugle calls and the ship's routine, and when 'action stations' sounded, he went like a shot from anywhere near a gun and hid under the lockers, only to emerge when he was quite certain it was all clear.

When the ship paid off, Minus found a good home with the family of one of the sailors. We often wondered how he liked Civvy Street, after being A.B. Minus R.N. for such a long time. While on board, his favourite pastime was chasing seagulls when they settled on the rails, and he'd jump so fiercely at them that he almost went over the top himself. Minus even had a little lifebelt made for him. He was a much-loved pussycat who'd certainly seen a lot of action.

21

MILESTONES

The great cauldron of war in Europe, fuelled by Nazism and stirred by the grasping hand of Hitler, was coming to the boil and the resulting splashes hit back at the cooks of that unholy brew. Things really began to change after three great men – Churchill, Roosevelt and Stalin – met in Teheran and cooked up another recipe: one that would have the taste of freedom and liberation. Plans were made for the greatest amphibious landing that had ever been attempted: the D-Day invasion of Europe, which commenced on 6 June 1944. 4,000 ships took part in this colossal operation, in which brave men showed what the Allied Forces were made of. The tide had now turned and we were on the offensive at last. History was being made and much detail has been recorded of this epic triumph that ultimately led to the liberation of millions of people and a milestone in everyone's life.

We had a little family milestone of our own, with Tom at home when leave permitted, for he was studying again and, as before, promotion was the objective. This time, he was aiming to leave the lower deck. He was shuttling between Chatham and Portsmouth, going through various departments for advancement, including Diving School, Navigation, Fire Fighting, Theory of Gunnery, Organisation and Officer-like qualities. When the course was over and the exams happily passed, I was a proud wife to see him come home in his brand new Officer's (Lieutenant) uniform, and I like to think that I played a little part in the study, as I had in his advancement during the immediate pre-war years.

By 12 June, the first V1 (doodlebug) unmanned aircraft fell on England. These devilish weapons meant yet more devastation for the innocent man and woman in the street, in their homes and the factories. My own sister Mabel fell foul of these terrible 'vengeance' weapons one awful night with her family, while sleeping peacefully in a farmhouse near Pluckley in Kent. The house was situated next to a shed that housed two bulls, which were both tethered in chains. The V1 fell and the

Jessie's elder sister, Mabel, who was trapped under rubble following a doodlebug attack on her home.

cottage collapsed all around them. They finally came-to, with rubble all over them and the house literally around their ears. But the worst terror came before they were rescued, as they heard the frightened bulls stamping and pulling at their chains, clearly as terrorised as the family was. In the darkness, they could not know if they would be trampled on by those crazed animals. Indeed, the realisation that the bulls could break their tethers, at any minute, alarmingly increased the terror felt by my poor trapped sister and her hapless family. Fortunately, they were dug out before such a thing could happen. They were bruised and bleeding, but mercifully none had been killed. Sadly though, they had lost their home and many of their belongings, and Mabel carried the mental scars of that night with her for the rest of her life.

The now homeless family were treated for their injuries and then given money for clothes and a rail ticket for Whitstable. I had no knowledge of the incident, until the afternoon of the 13th, when my sister and her son suddenly and unexpectedly turned up on my doorstep seeking shelter. The others had stayed behind to help salvage what could be rescued from the ruins of their former home. I was shocked to see them – my nephew John, aged twelve, still wearing a bloodstained shirt and his mother looking a complete wreck, hollow-eyed and somewhat hysterical. They were both still covered in glass splinters, which were continually coming to the surface over their bodies and in their hair.

I looked after them for a time, until they had made alternative arrangements, which enabled the family to be reunited under the same roof once more. However, I will never forget the account of that dreadful night, as related to me by a still deeply shocked Mabel: that all-too familiar drone of the doodlebug overhead, when the whole world seemed to be waiting for it to continue on its way. But then, there'd be that dreadful moment when the phut-phut sound of the engine ceased, followed by the nervous counting of the seconds, until that inevitable bang would come. And who was to know where it would fall? That night, my own family were the unlucky ones. [Editor's note: At about this time, the Hookhams moved from no. 15 Ellis Road, to a house opposite, at no. 30. Gran Vine and Aunt Polly – who died shortly afterwards – remained at no. 15. Bob Hookham tells me that they were soon joined, at no. 30, by his other grandmother, Maud Anne Hookham, who had moved up from Herne, and could no longer cope on her own.]

To all of us, even in the relative safety of Whitstable, the V1 seemed to be the ultimate in destructive weapons. However, on 8 September, the V2 rocket turned up with even more devastation. [Editor's note: Records show that at least one V2 rocket – then code-named 'Big Ben' – landed on the outskirts of Whitstable.]

A family group at no. 30 Ellis Road, Tankerton. Back row, left to right: Bob Hookham, Ivy Hookham and Ted Vine. Front row: Joy, Emily Vine (Gran), Doris (Ted's wife) and their daughter Anne.

22

PARIS LIBERATED

On 23 August, Paris was liberated. Back at home, hope ran high as a result, but the war was not over yet; there was still a long way to go. Winston Churchill went to the French capital for the celebrations, and representatives of all three British services followed to take part in the huge procession that had been arranged. Two Royal Navy officers (Tom being one of them) trained a guard of honour for the occasion. They travelled to Paris via Newhaven and Dieppe, passing the appalling debris and wreckage of war as they went by road through villages and towns. En route, they certainly saw sights never to be forgotten.

The grand parade was a somewhat circuitous route via the Champs Elysées to the Arc de Triomphe. Crowds lined the streets and the British were cheered and fêted all the way, showing a genuine feeling of relief to see them. [Editor's note: This was the second high-profile occasion that my grandfather had been asked to participate in. As I have already mentioned in the introduction, he'd been one of the many such men who had pulled the gun carriage bearing the coffin of George V at his state funeral.]

The two Naval officers, with Tom second-in-command, led the columns of sailors with bayonets and swords at the carry, all the way, changing arms at intervals. Carrying a sword in this manner is very tiring on the arms and, at the finish, quite excruciating when relaxing the arm at last. Nevertheless, they were filled with pride by the reception they received throughout the procession.

There was also a grand ceremonial occasion when the Great Hall was lined with soldiers of the French Guard with their plumed steel helmets. There were also many speeches! After the procession, the two officers were given a car and a chauffeur at their disposal; to take them round Paris and they had a never-to-be-forgotten tour of all the famous sights of the capital. When it was finally all over, Tom carried home with him many wonderful memories of the special hospitality of the French people.

Back at home again, it was the bitterly cold winter of 1944/5 and as we sparingly placed the coal on the fire, we thought of the Bevan Boys: those young men – often from privileged backgrounds – aged between eighteen and twenty-five, who had been diverted to the mining industry a year before.

Time passed for us in very much the same pattern as before the Liberation of Paris, and we were feeling so very glad that we'd decided to stay in the Whitstable area. It was as safe as anywhere could be, but many other areas around London were having an especially dreadful time now that the V2s were coming over even more frequently. Hitler must have known that the V2 rockets could do little to turn the tide of war back in his favour, so they were vengeance-only weapons, pure and simple.

So pleased to have her Daddy back home again! Joy sits on Tom's knee, just before bedtime, at no. 71 Wynn Road.

Reunited at last! Tom and Jessie relax together in the front room of no. 71, in the final months of the war.

In April of 1945, we heard, with great sadness, of the death of President Roosevelt. He was a true friend to the British people, and his name will never be forgotten. And then more heartening news came when it was announced that the Russia and Americans had linked up in Germany. Later in the same month, the world was shocked by the ignominious death of the Italian leader (Mussolini) and his mistress. Tyrant he certainly was, but what a dreadful way to end two lives. Two days later, Hitler and his new wife of a few hours, Eva Braun, died deplorable deaths at their own hands, and the world shed no tears for them.

Finally, enemy forces in north-west Germany, Holland and Denmark surrendered to the Allies, and the end of the Second World War was officially declared to take effect from one minute to midnight on 8 May 1945.

23

THE PEACE PAGEANT

Even though war with the other axis power, Japan, was still going on, we in Britain had a public holiday to celebrate the peace in Europe. At the same time, thousands of servicemen were released to find their way back to Civvy Street, which, in many cases, did not turn out to be an easy task. Even so, for a short while, as Churchill encouraged, the population let go all their pent-up tensions and were happy that it was finally all over at this side of the world. However, many still grieved for their loved ones who were fighting the Japanese enemy, or were being so cruelly held prisoner.

Some progress towards a peacetime way-of-life could now be made. The hated blackout curtains came down, the lights went on again, the church bells were rung as before hostilities, and there were bonfires lit all over the country. Street parties were being held in many areas, where nearly everybody managed to turn out miracles of confection from the existing rations. Even the ubiquitous Spam sandwiches never tasted so good! There was also dancing in the street – I remained an enthusiastic observer – while laughing, crying hysterical people linked arms with strangers, as can only happen on occasions such as this.

Other signs of war took far longer to remove. The lengths of barbed wire, which had cut off our Whitstable beaches, from Swalecliffe to Seasalter, would remain for some months to come; the threatened invasion they were installed to repel now but a distant memory.

Throughout this post-VE Day period, I was still helping out at the P.N.E.U. School, but we would soon break up for the end of term, and the long school summer holiday. The principal, Miss Proctor, asked the staff to think up ideas for a show, preferably a pageant with a patriotic theme, which would capture the national mood of celebration and peace.

During the following weekend, while I was frying sausages – which I'd heard described as 'breadcrumbs in battledress' – I thought of all those people from all walks of life who had made VE Day possible. As I turned the sausages over, a couple of verses of a suitable poem quickly came to me. Late on, I continued until there were eighteen verses in all. [Editor's note: In actual fact, nineteen verses were written and performed.] On the following Monday, I presented these to Miss Proctor, along with the rest of the staff, and I was proud to hear that they were unanimously accepted and would form the soundtrack around which our pageant would be staged.

The event turned out to be a huge success and every child had a part to play. It was quite touching and many people in the audience showed signs of being affected by those recent wartime memories being depicted by the little ones. [Editor's note: The pageant took place in All Saints' Hall, next to the old church, in Church Street. My grandmother played the piano in a portion of the proceedings, and my mother played the part of an evacuee.]

The coastal defences at Seasalter (west of Whitstable) in 1945, still in place and, thankfully, never needed.

Not what it seems! A defensive pillbox, cleverly disguised as a beach attendant's hut, on the apron between Tankerton and Whitstable. Whitstable harbour can just be seen in the distance.

The following is an extract from the *Whitstable Times*, of 27 July 1945:

Then came the Victory Pageant, clever and colourful. Very much trouble must have been taken in the production and in procuring and making the costumes. It opened by showing Britannia on the stage, with four representative attendants, who spoke the touching words written by Mrs Vine. Britannia looked delightfully dignified and impressive. At a given signal, she raised her shield, disclosing Mr Churchill's portrait amid great applause and, as the poem unfolded, each section of the Army, Navy, Air Force and Civil Defences – all dressed for their various occupations – together with all the Allied countries waving flags, marched up the hall to the sound of suitable music, accompanied by a drum.

The Allied countries made a most colourful group. They all marched up the hall in the following order: Army, Navy, Air Force, Land army, Firewatchers, Ambulance men, Doctors and nurses, Policeman, Miner, Salvage man, Factory workers, Dig for Victory, mothers and evacuees, and then the Allied countries. To the sound of the patriotic song 'Land of Hope and Glory', the groups of little actors, dressed in their colourful costumes, stood on the platform under the Churchill picture and sang as if their hearts would burst. Then – 'God save the King'. All the children were splendid and took it all quite seriously, especially the prayer for the fallen, which came just before the end. The march past was most effective and really moving, and made a victorious end to a delightful afternoon.

The Pageant Poem

> We'll tell you a simple story,
> In a simple sort of way,
> Of Britain's sons and daughters,
> Who won for us VE Day.*
>
> They came from every quarter,
> From cottage and farm and hall,
> And stood with grim resolution,
> When backs were against the wall.
>
> They rallied around the standard,
> When hope was nearly gone,
> Amid trial and tribulation,
> Not one of them looked forlorn.
>
> They showed an heroic spirit,
> The rest of the world admired,
> And looked to a mighty leader,
> Whom God Himself inspired.
>
> He made no eloquent promise,
> 'Mid fanfares, drums and cheers,
> But told us to do our duty,
> With 'blood and sweat and tears.'
>
> They knew the path of duty,
> They heard the clarion call,
> Wives and sisters, husbands, sons,
> Were ready to fight or fall.

* Editor's note: My grandmother omitted this first verse, in her typed manuscript, but I have restored it from the original 1945 record, for the sake of completeness.

The boys who were dressed in khaki,
The sailor men in blue,
And the RAF – a gallant band,
Strove hard to pull us through.

Woman worked shoulder to shoulder,
With men at the factory bench,
Hands that were meant for loving tasks,
Were blistered with hammer and wrench.

In workmanlike breeches and leggings,
Our women worked on the land,
At tasks that hitherto men had done,
The effort they made was grand.

The slogan was 'Dig for Victory',
To lighten the merchantmen's toil,
We all began digging our gardens,
Producing the food from the soil.

Some of them trained as wardens,
Some for the fire-watch teams,
The rescue squad were ever alert,
When sirens shattered our dreams.

We all had to learn about salvage,
The paper and rags and bones,
Men and women and children too,
Collected it from their homes.

We remember the doctors and nurses,
Their courage, devotion and skill.
The Red Cross post and the stretcher men,
How nobly they worked with a will.

The mothers we're going to mention,
Who merit a deal of praise,
In unspectacular work at home,
They helped in countless ways.

They did wonders with family rations,
They toiled at the mend and make-do,
They knitted and sewed for evacuees,
For soldiers and sailors too.

We mustn't forget the policeman,
His duties were never done,
And the lads who had to go down the mines,
Away from the light of the sun.

There's many more worthy of mention,
Who earned our undying thanks,
In defence of a country's honour,
Stood valiant in the ranks.

We pay homage to all the heroes,
The men who are England's pride.
We remember the thousands, who'll never return,
For England and home they died.

We salute our gallant Allies,
And friends across the sea,
They gave their all in freedom's name,
For peace and Democracy.

24

WHAT HAPPENED NEXT

by Paul Crampton

In late 1944, or early 1945, having achieved the officer rank of lieutenant, my grandfather transferred to HMS *Frobisher*, which served as an officer cadet training ship. As gunnery was his speciality, this was the skill he taught mainly. In fact, one Philip Mountbatten – later to become the Duke of Edinburgh – was one of his pupils during the mid-1940s. The *Frobisher* was a 'Hawkins' Class heavy-cruiser, launched in 1920, and had become obsolete in design long before the Second World War. The HMS *Vindictive*, on which Tom served immediately prior to the war, was a sister ship of the *Frobisher*, but the former had been converted into a training ship in the 1930s, and was therefore very different in appearance by this time.

Being an old ship, HMS *Frobisher* had been mothballed prior to hostilities, but shipping losses and shortages forced its reinstatement and refit in January 1940. Having been torpedoed by German U-boats in June 1944, the ship was repaired, partly disarmed, and then converted into a cadet training ship.

For my grandfather, the elderly *Frobisher* must have quite a contrast to the brand-new *Euryalus* on which he'd served for a large part of the war, but he always recalled it as a very happy ship, with polite cadets, all only too keen to listen and learn. He did at least three tours of duty aboard HMS *Frobisher*, as the world got used to peace once more:

Autumn Cruise 1945 – (8 September to 23 November) taking in Spithead, Scilly Isles, Ullapool, Greenock, Salen, Holyhead, Mount's Bay (Penzance), Torquay, Plymouth, Gibraltar, Valletta (Malta), Gibraltar and Portsmouth.

Spring Cruise 1946 – (4 January to 28 March) taking in Portsmouth, Gibraltar, Trinidad (Pointe-à-Pierre), Port of Spain, Grenada, Barbados, Dominica (Roseau), Dominica (Portsmouth), Antigua, St Lucia, Jamaica (Kingston), Jamaica (Montego Bay), Port of Spain, Barbados, Gibraltar and Portsmouth.

Summer Cruise 1946 – (3 May to 1 August), taking in Portsmouth, Penzance, Falmouth, Plymouth, Holyhead, Portree, Ullapool, Rosyth, Oslo, Copenhagen, Göteborg, Rosyth and Portsmouth (for examinations, prize giving and then cadets' leave).

HMS *Frobisher*, probably at Portsmouth, in the immediate post-war period.

The fact that HMS *Frobisher* was such a happy ship is clearly demonstrated by this anonymous poem that appeared in the ship's magazine for the Autumn Cruise of 1945.

A WARDROOM ALPHABET

A stands for Archdale, the white hope of Whaley,
He reads through the Gunnery Drill Book twice daily.

B is for Belsen, which is generally reckoned
To run the old *Frobie* a pretty good second.

C's slipped my mind, I regret to confess –
It's for something discussed quite a lot in the mess.

D's the despair that we feel when the rain
Compels us to cancel Divisions again.

E is for editor – a glorious job –
Forty-eight pages of tripe for three bob.

F's for the F'xle – very much to the fore
(geographically speaking, of course – nothing more).

G stands for Giffard, for Gregg and for Gore,
And also for Gin – I need hardly say more.

H stands for – Careful, be very polite,
You know who H stands for? Gorblimey, too right.

I is a thing which one never forgets –
The Impression that we must make on the cadets.

J stands for Jago, who'll thank you a lot
For a nice cup of cocoa made up in the Plot.

K is for Keyham, that strangest of schools
Where they teach the young plumbers to go back for their tools.

L is for Lethargy, hard to condemn,
That falls on instructional classes p.m.

M is a Matter best left undiscussed –
Where Marryat goes when he's off on the bust.

N is for Noisy the Novol (P. One),
Not to worry's his motto. Let's all have some fun.

O's what I'll get at the end of the cruise
When they come to assessing me for O.L.Qs.

P is for Pontius – an equal success
At sea on the bridge or at bridge in the mess.

Q is the Quarterdeck, blazing with light,
Like the fun fair at Pompey on Saturday night.

R's my Release group – seventy odd;
By the time they reach me, I'll be under the sod.

S is the Senior, so supple and slim.
Quasi-permanent's not the description for him.

T's for the Talkies we have once a week –
The programmes this cruise must be nearly unique.

U is for Ullapool. I've got my suspicion
There's some great attraction there other than fishin'.

V's the Vulgarity which daily gets wusser
In the habits and speech of a certain young pusser.

W's watchkeepers – about to collapse –
One watch in eight comes so hard on the chaps.

X is an officer best left unnamed –
His behaviour makes even the Major ashamed.

Y is too hard and the same goes for Z.
Let's drop all this nonsense and go home to bed.

The old ship was finally sold for scrap in March 1949, and was broken up at Newport two months later. During this same period, my grandmother decided to acquire yet another skill, and began helping out at a hairdresser's shop in Tankerton Road, near the Wynn Road junction. After school, my mother would go and watch the various cutting and hairdressing procedures, as Jessie became ever more proficient. From that moment onwards, and for almost the rest of her life, my grandmother always did the family haircuts, thus saving everyone a lot of money over the years.

Tom Vine finally resigned from the Navy on his fortieth birthday, 19 January 1947, having served the twenty-five years he'd originally signed up for. Well-meaning colleagues offered him several very lucrative Civil Service-type jobs in London, but my grandfather had something completely different in mind. Having survived the war, against the odds, and also having missed his family – as well as a large part of my mother's upbringing – he felt a desperate need to get back to basics once more. Initially, he trained as a watch and clock repairer, working from home. Skilled brother-in-law Reg Grime (husband of Jessie's younger sister Grace) gave him some much-needed tutoring and, by all accounts, work came flooding in. My mother remembers being so fascinated seeing this big man, with his big fingers, handle such delicate components and mechanisms.

Before long though, being cooped up inside all the time was rapidly losing its appeal. Tom wanted all the benefits of a home life, and having his family close by, but he wanted to get out into the fresh air; he wanted to work with nature and make his living in an even simpler way.

Adjusting to life on Civvy Street. Tom with his sister Ivy, Jessie and Joy, in the late 1940s.

So it was that my grandfather retrained as a horticulturalist, taking a postal night-school type course, in order to become qualified in all matters green-fingered. Inevitably, my grandmother keenly involved herself in this new direction of learning – very much as she had done with his Navy promotional courses – and, as a result, learnt as much about horticulture and gardening as he did!

In the meantime though, a living had to be earned, so Tom went to work for local nurseryman, Charlie Hunt, who also happened to be their landlord at no. 71 Wynn Road. My grandfather helped to establish Frank Brown Nursery, at several locations off Ham Shades Lane, in the late 1940s. The main part of this nursery was based on the area now occupied by the appropriately named Nursery Close.

One of his most memorable, not to mention back-breaking, tasks during this period, was to plant, by hand, many thousands of daffodil bulbs in fields now occupied by Fox Grove Road (now you know why these springtime flowers are so profuse in the gardens of that area!). At this time, Nacholt Nursery in Ham Shades Lane, was also part of the 'Frank Brown' complex (owned by Mr Hunt) and it specialised in bedding plants, hence the extremely long greenhouse that many will remember at this location.

During the late 1940s, Jessie was also doing her bit to bring in a little bit of extra money. She regularly contributed both articles and poems to the *Whitstable Times*, some of which were based on their personal experience at the time. One of her poems appeared as part of an advert for Frank Brown Nursery. It went as follows:

'CAPABILITY' BROWN

Across the bridge at Tankerton,
and near the shops in town.
A firm of good and sound repute,
Is 'Horticulture Brown'.

Potted plants of every kind,
flowers of renown.
Vegetables superior
by 'Enterprising Brown'.

Bedding plants in boxes,
which never cause a frown.
You'll always say you're glad you went
to 'Dedicated Brown'.

Tomatoes are perfection,
in clusters hanging down.
We'll aim to grow the very best
Says 'Conscientious Brown'.

For decorating stages and
adorning beauty's crown.
For best bouquets and buttonholes,
try 'Floral Artist Brown'.

As Joy got older, it became more and more obvious that she was developing some digestive problems, especially with things made of flour, such as bread or scones. It was then that my grandmother remembered those earlier wartime trips over to Blean Woods in order to gather chestnuts. Therefore, in the autumn, the trips resumed and, having got her booty home, Jessie would peel the nuts and then ground them into a sort of flour substitute with which she was able to bake things, and these proved far more digestible to my mother. My grandfather stoically helped in the chestnut-peeling sessions, and also ate the products that were produced as a result. Later on though, he confessed to a male confidant, 'we're eating so many bloomin' chestnuts that we're beginning to look like them!'

While chestnuts were plentiful in the war years and the immediate post-war period, there was something else that my mother very much enjoyed that could not be got – even if the average person could afford them at the time – and that was fireworks. Traditionally let off on 5 November, and not for any other trivial reason (as seems to be the case today), fireworks were never seen in the shops during the wartime years. However, from 1945 onwards, it became obvious that one particular house in Pier Avenue – which ran parallel to Wynn Road – did indeed have access to fireworks and were putting on a good display. Ever keen to seek an opportunity, Joy decided to sneak along the 10ft alleyway, which divided the back gardens of each respective street, and proceeded to peer through gaps in their back fence in order to enjoy the display. This covert operation became an annual event – sometimes, cousin Bob was even dragged along to watch too – and, as far as we can tell, the firework-obtaining family never knew of their secret observer.

Apparently, this was not my mother's only covert operation undertaken during this period. In the early months of the war (if not just before), Mr Hunt had built a communal air raid shelter for the occupants of the bungalows he owned at the bottom end of Wynn Road. Constructed of brick with a flat concrete roof, this substantial structure stood at the bottom of the garden at no. 73, next door to my grandparents' place (no. 73 was occupied by a Mrs Piper, a Naval widow who had lost her husband at sea, on one of the big RN ship s that had gone down with few survivors). Little used, if at all, by the end of the war years, the shelter had become partly obscured by the overhanging branches of an old almond tree. Ever keen to extend her rations, my mother soon found a way of climbing from her back garden, onto the flat roof of the shelter. And there, completely hidden by the overhanging branches, she would crack open the almonds with a hammer – using the concrete flat roof of the shelter – and feast on the nuts until she'd had sufficient.

As for my mother's schooling, she continued at the P.N.E.U. until its untimely closure in about 1947, and then transferred to another local private school called Dunelm. She subsequently passed the eleven-plus exam, but was unable to find a position at the Simon Langton Girls' Grammar School in Canterbury (the school had been all-but wiped out in the June 1942 Blitz, on its Whitefriars site in Canterbury, and was currently based at a former asylum on the outskirts of the city). After an unhappy two weeks at Faversham Grammar, my mother settled at the Whitstable Endowed School, until leaving at the age of fifteen, just before Christmas 1950.

In the early 1950s, Jessie went to work for Lefevre's Department Store in Canterbury, in the fabric department. Joy joined her there on 27 December 1950, virtually straight from school, as an apprentice window dresser. My mother stayed for about three years before becoming a telephonist, at the Stour Street Exchange, Canterbury. However, she found the constant sitting down a problem, and left in August 1953. Her next career move was also a temporary one. She actually joined the Navy (the WRNS) and was based at the Naval Training College in Reading, Berkshire. This was obviously a move following in her father's footsteps, but this legacy proved somewhat of a millstone and, besides, she began to miss the young man she'd recently begun dating back in Canterbury.

Joy had met Dave Crampton, at the Stour Street Exchange, as he was a telephone engineer. They'd also bumped into each other at a lot of local dances. The blossoming relationship was enough to bring her back into Civvy Street, and a job working at Finlay's Tobacconist, no. 1 Mercery Lane, Canterbury.

In 1955, all those years of scrimping and saving finally paid off and my grandparents were able to purchase Nacholt Nursery from Mr Hunt, and set up on their own. The nursery came with a cottage (Nacholt) and 1½ acres of land that was already in use as part of the nursery complex.

Tom, with 'Frank Brown's' familiar old grey tractor, in the main drive of Nacholt Nursery, in Ham Shades Lane, Tankerton. The roof of Rosario can be seen in the background.

The new Vine family home, Nacholt, in 1955, just after redecorating, and the installation of the conservatory. Joy quietly embroiders in the recently completed structure.

Joy, having just married Dave Crampton, at All Saints' Church, in March 1956.

Paul and Lois Crampton, in the back garden of Rosario, in about 1963, with Nacholt Nursery, and the long tomato greenhouse, in the background.

Bedding plants were continued by the new owners, but to this were added tomatoes, cucumbers, fruit from their modest on-site orchard, eggs and many cut flowers, especially chrysanthemums, freesias and dahlias. The cut flowers were sold on to Ivy and Sid Hookham who had, by this time, purchased a flower shop, with a flat above, in nearby Tankerton High Street.

Tom continued to do favours for Charlie Hunt, when his specialist skills were needed and, in return, Grandad was allowed to borrow the Frank Brown Nursery's grey tractor whenever he needed it.

On 24 March 1956, Joy and Dave were married from Nacholt. The ceremony took place at All Saints' Church in nearby Church Street. They bought their first home at no. 18 Crown Gardens, Canterbury. I was born there in October 1957, and my sister Lois in November 1959.

When Lois was barely two weeks old, our family moved to a bungalow called Rosario in Ham Shades Lane, which happened to be right next door to Nacholt Nursery. Personally, I recall those pre-schools years, with Nacholt Nursery as my private playground, as among the happiest times of my life. In December 1963, the family moved back to Canterbury, to make my father's travelling to and from work much easier. My grandparents hung on at Nacholt Nursery until a developer made them an offer they couldn't refuse, in 1965. Nacholt Close covers the site today, although the original bungalow still survives among the plush 1960s houses.

Tom and Jessie Vine, outside their bungalow in Gainsborough Drive, Beltinge, during 1977, at the time of the launch of their illustrated book of fishing poems *Hook, Line and Sinker*. *(Courtesy of the Kentish Gazette)*

Widows in later life, Jessie Vine and Ivy Hookham together for the final time, and both well into their nineties.

My grandparents then moved to Rodmersham, near Sittingbourne, and Grandad became head gardener to the Doubleday family. Our family followed them in 1966, and purchased a house in the adjacent village of Bapchild. My younger brother Tom was born while we were here, in April 1967. Having lost her beloved Tom in 1991, my grandmother continued to live in retirement in both Herne and Beltinge, near Herne Bay, and finally died at Laylam retirement home, on 19 December 2002, aged ninety-five.

My parents, Joy and Dave, also live in retirement in Beltinge. In recent years, my mother has followed in another of her late father's footsteps, namely by displaying an aptitude for art. She has very much developed her own style, and even has her own online art gallery: www.joycramptonart.co.uk

APPENDIX

TOM VINE
A WHITSTABLE MAN'S WAR

The life and times of HMS *Euryalus*

(All reproduced from contemporary and original documentation).

1941

16 September – Sailed from Greenock (in Scotland): the base for the Home Fleet and assembly point for Convoy Ships.

21 September – Entered the Mediterranean via Gibraltar with a convoy for Malta.

29 September – Arrived at Malta with convoy after numerous engagements with enemy aircraft. Sailed P.M. for Gibraltar.

1 October – Left the Mediterranean via Gibraltar.

8 October – Arrived at Freetown (Sierra Leone) and sailed for St Helena.

14 October – Arrived at St Helena and sailed for Simon's Town.

19 October – *Euryalus* arrived at Simon's Town (the Naval Base in South Africa).

28 October – Sailed for Mombasa (Kenya).

3 November – Arrived at Mombasa and sailed for Aden (Yemen).

7 November – Arrived at Aden and sailed for Alexandria.

11 November – Arrived at Alexandria and the joined the 15th Cruiser Squadron.

HMS *Euryalus* in camouflage colours at sea during 1941.

18 November – Concentration bombardment with HMS *Naiad* (a sister 'Dido' class cruiser to the *Euryalus*) against Halfaya Pass (in Egypt, near the border with Libya). This was the start of the Eighth Army's 1941 offensive.

21 November to 2 December – Operations in company with the 15th Cruiser Squadron.

8 December – General operations.

10 December – *Euryalus* returned to Alexandria.

13 to 18 December – Malta Convoy.

1942
5 to 9 January – Malta Convoy.

16 to 20 January – Malta Convoy.

24 to 28 January – Escorted HMS *Cleopatra* (another 'Dido' class cruiser) from Malta to Alexandria.

12 to 16 February – Malta Convoy.

10 to 12 March – General Operations.

14 March – Carried out bombardment of Rhodes Island (Dodecanese – Greek islands).

HMS *Euryalus* in action. A nearby ship is hit in the stern.

20 March – Sailed from Alexandria with Convoy for Malta.

22 March – Engagement with the Italian Fleet, which tried to intercept the convoy. [There is a detailed account of this engagement towards the end of the appendix]

24 March – Arrived at Alexandria and changed 5.25in gun barrels.

13 to 16 June – Malta Convoy (forced by powerful enemy surface and air forces to return to Alexandria).

28 June – Escorted HMS *Queen Elizabeth* to Port Said (following lengthy repairs to it at Alexandria – the ship had been mined at Alexandria in December 1941).

29 June – Evacuated Alexandria.

19 July – Bombarded Mersa Matruh (a seaport in Egypt).

22 July – Further bombardment of Mersa Matruh.

10 August – Patrolling off Alexandria (disturbance with Vichy French warships).

12 August – *Euryalus* returned to Port Said (Egypt).

15 August – Sailed for Haifa (Palestine/Israel).

4 September – Sailed for Massawa (on the Red Sea coast) and arrived 6 September for docking. 48 hours leave to visit Asmara, capital of Italian Eritrea.

13 September – Sailed for Port Said.

15 September – Arrived at Port Said and hoisted the flag of the 15th Cruiser Squadron (Rear Admiral A.J. Power).

19 September – *Euryalus* sailed for Haifa.

30 September – Sailed for Port Said.

2 October – Hauled down the flag of the 15th Cruiser Squadron.

16 October – Sailed and arrived at Port Suez (at the southern boundary of the canal in Egypt).

17 to 24 October – Acted as Guard Ship at Anchorage 'B'.

25 October – Sailed to and arrived at Port Suez.

28 October – Sailed to and arrived at Port Said.

7 to 8 November – Operations (acting as decoy during the passage of the Convoy to Malta from Gibraltar).

16 November – Sailed on General Operations.

20 November – Arrived at Malta with stores for the island.

21 November – Sailed for Alexandria, arrived on 23 November.

25 November – Sailed for Malta with more stores, arrived on 27 November.

3 December – Sailed on operations (escorted convoy to Malta).

13 December – Operations with the 15th Cruiser Squadron.

28 to 31 December – Italian Fleet reported at sea (no contact).

1943
22 January – Concentration bombardment with HMS *Cleopatra* against Zuara, near Tripoli in Libya. [Please see the end of the appendix for more details of this particular operation]

8 to 10 February – Shipping sweep (mine/enemy ship clearance). Axis evacuation of Tunisia.

21 March – Sailed for docking at Alexandria, arrived 23 March.

14 April – Sailed and arrived at Port Suez, operating until 19 April with the RAF.

20 April – Sailed for Alexandria.

21 April – Arrived at Alexandria and then sailed for Malta.

23 April – *Euryalus* arrived at Malta.

8 June – Bombarded Pantelleria (an island in the Strait of Sicily), and then proceeded to and arrive at Bone [?].

21 June – Sailed for Algiers and arrived on 22 June.

6 July – Sailed for the planned Invasion of Sicily (Force 'H').

8 July – Oiled at Tripoli. [Presumably taking on fuel]

10 July – Commenced the Invasion of Sicily.

12 July – Oiled at Malta.

18 July – Returned to Malta. Operations completed.

20 July – Sailed for Bone and arrived 21 July.

31 July – Sailed on General Operations.

HMS *Euryalus* in action. A very near miss is observed by a crew member.

1 August – Bombarded Vibo Valentia (in Italy).

11 August – Sailed for Bizerta (Tunisia) – arrived 12 August.

16 August – Sailed on General Operations.

17 August Arrived at Palermo, then sailed and bombarded Scalea (both in Italy).

18 August – Arrived at Malta.

26 August – Sailed for Algiers (the capital of Algeria).

27 August – Arrived at Algiers and hoisted the flag of Rear-Admiral Force 'V' (Sir Phillip Vian). Afterwards, sailed for Gibraltar.

28 August – Arrived at Gibraltar.

29 August – *Euryalus* at sea exercising with Force 'V'.

30 August – sailed for Algiers, arrived 31 August.

5 September – Sailed for Malta.

8 September – Sailed on operations with Force 'V'. Armistice with the Italian government was announced while passing through the Straits of Messina (between Sicily and Italy).

9 September – Commenced assault on the Gulf of Salerno (off south-west Italy).

12 September – Force 'V' operations completed. Arrived at Palermo.

13 September – Sailed for, and arrived at Bizerta (Tunisia).

14 September – Sailed for Tripoli, and embarked with troops on board.

15 September – Arrived at Salerno beaches with the troops.

16 September – Sailed from Salerno, escorting HMS *Warspite* (a 'Queen Elizabeth' class battleship from 1915). The ship was badly damaged, having been hit by three guided missiles from German aircraft – 9 killed and 14 wounded).

19 September – Left HMS *Warspite* (in the care of US Navy tugs) and arrived at Bizerta (captain changed command). Sailed for Salerno.

20 September – Arrived at Salerno. Patrolling beaches.

21 September – Sailed for, and arrived at Malta.

22 September – Hoisted the flag of the Commander-in-Chief (Admiral of the Fleet, Sir Andrew Cunningham), and proceeded to Taranto (southern Italy).

23 September – Hauled down flag and sailed for Malta.

24 September – *Euryalus* arrived at Malta.

27 September – Sailed for Algiers.

28 September – Arrived, and then sailed from Algiers, with Colonel Knox (Secretary of the US Navy) and his staff to Bizerta.

29 September – Arrived at Bizerta. Disembarked Colonel Knox and then sailed for Algiers.

30 September – Arrived back at Algiers. Received signal to proceed to the UK for a refit and to give leave. Loud and prolonged cheers!

1 October – Sailed for Gibraltar.

2 October – Arrived at Gibraltar and then sailed for the UK.

MESSAGE

'Euryalus'   C. in C. Med

On the departure of 'HMS Euryalus' from the Station, I wish you all a Happy Homecoming and I shall be glad to see you back on the Station. 'Euryalus' leaves the Med. with a fine record; she has taken part in every operation of importance during the last 2 years and has always acquitted herself with distinction. It was a great regret to me that circumstances prevented me from coming on-board before the ship sailed, to wish you all goodbye.

011832A

REPLY

Your 011832A. Thank you for your message, which is much appreciated by all on-board.

020856A

2 October 1943.

The pentagonal crest of HMS *Euryalus*, the five-side shape denoting a cruiser.

HMS 'Euryalus'   30th March 1942.

GUNNERY NARRATIVE OF THE SURFACE ACTION AGAINST THE ITALIAN FLEET ON 22nd MARCH 1942

1: - What was believed to be smoke from enemy surface ships was sighted and reported by 'Euryalus' at 14:08 bearing 353 degrees. At 14:24, three ships were sighted by 'Euryalus' and reported bearing 015 degrees. 'Cleopatra' and 'Euryalus' (currently escorting a convoy) altered to starboard to close the enemy and at 14:53, started to make smoke (i.e. to lay down a 'smoke-screen' to conceal the ship and therefore make enemy targeting of it more difficult).

2: - At 14:55, the first enemy shells were observed to fall ahead of 'Cleopatra'. The enemy ships in sight, which consisted of three cruisers, at this time bore 009 degrees. At 14:56, 'Cleopatra' opened fire in concentration with 'Euryalus', 'Cleopatra' being Master Ship. At 14:59, 'Euryalus' was ordered to take Master Ship, the target being the third cruiser visible from the right. Firing at maximum range continued until 15:07, when 'Cleopatra' ordered, 'check fire' (i.e. to stop firing). During this part of the engagement, the observation of fall of shot was extremely difficult owing to the long range, the hazy conditions due to spray blown up by the high wind, and the smoke screen being laid by 'Cleopatra' and 'Euryalus'. Shortly after 15:00, the enemy withdrew to the Northward.

3: - At about 15:18, (our) course was altered to 235 degrees and the convoy was rejoined at 16:05.

4: - At 16:38, the enemy ships were again sighted by 'Euryalus', bearing 035 degrees. 'Cleopatra' altered to 010 degrees and 'Euryalus' followed.

5: - At 16:43, one battleship was sighted from the bridge and reported bearing 037 degrees, and at 16:44 a 15-inch salvo fell near 'Cleopatra'. At the same time, 'Cleopatra' and 'Euryalus' opened fire in individuals ship control. During this period of the engagement, some snap ranges of targets were obtained as they came in view through gaps in the smoke screen. These ranges varied between 19,400 yards and 18,500 yards. Each time, the ranges were tuned-to in the T.S. and deflection groups fired. At 16:44, 'Cleopatra' and 'Euryalus' started to make smoke again and continued doing so for the remainder of the action. This naturally greatly interfered with control and spotting procedure.

6: - At 16:49, it was observed that 'Cleopatra's W/T (wireless/telegraphy) aerials were shot away and, at about this same time, 'Euryalus; was hit by a splinter in the after superstructure from a near miss of a 15-inch shell. During this period, 'Euryalus' fired a few salvos on a target compass bearing 290 degrees and a range of 20,000 yards, signalled by 'Cleopatra', as 'Euryalus' was unable to see any targets owing to the smoke screen.

HMS *Euryalus* in action: a depth charge goes off, with a heavy smoke screen in the background.

7: - At 17:14, (our) own course was 270 degrees, with the convoy on the Port beam. At 17:20, the convoy was ordered to steam south. At 17:30, (our) own course was altered to 090 degrees.

8: - From time to time, the forward group was changed back to H.A. Control when no surface targets were being engaged, and aircraft attacks were either being made or were imminent.

9: - At 18:05, R.D.F. Type 284 (radio direction finder) obtained the range of a target at 16,000 yards, bearing 320 degrees. This fact was reported to 'Cleopatra' by W/T. The target was (on) the other side of the smoke screen. A number of Zig-Zag groups were fired centred on R.D.F. ranges, though the target did not become visible until 18:39. Gyro firing was used at the director. At 18:39, what was thought to be an enemy cruiser came in sight bearing 285 degrees at an R.D.F. range of 14,000 yards. This target remained visible sufficiently clearly for 'Euryalus' to fire a total of 21 6-gun salvos at it. R.D.F. Type 284 ranges were used throughout and Zig-Zag groups centred on the R.D.F. range were fired. A few definitive straddles were observed and it is thought that some direct hits were obtained on this target. The lowest range obtained at this time was 11,200 yards. At 18:56, a column of smoke was observed rising from the enemy (thus confirming damage), and at 19:00, (our) own course was altered to 100 degrees and the surface engagement was concluded.

10: - It will thus be seen that the surface engagement took place in three separate phases as far as 'Euryalus' was concerned, namely (1) 14:56 to 15:07, (2) 16:44 to 17:30 and (3) 18:05 to 19:00.

11: - Owing to the conditions, very few splashes of Low Angle Shell were observed throughout the whole engagement, and most of the time the actual targets were difficult to make out.

12: - A total of 421 5.25-inch S.A.P. (semi-armour-piercing) rounds were fired, i.e. 70 rounds per gun from the forward group. The after group was employed continuously in engaging aircraft, which threatened or attacked. At 17:33 one aircraft was shot down by 'Euryalus'. The aircraft exploded on hitting the water. It is not known how many 5.25-inch H.E. (high explosive) rounds were fired at aircraft during the surface action, but a total of 1097 rounds were fired during the whole operation.

A report by Harry Crockett (Associated Press Naval Correspondent)

ABOARD THE BRITISH CRUISER HMS 'EURYALUS' OFF TRIPOLITANIA,
22nd JANUARY 1943

Zuara, Tripoli – waterfront railroad terminus and jumping-off place for Rommel's backpedalling forces – rocked and blazed furiously early today as British warships showered it with tons of high explosives in a surprise, close range bombardment.

The full extent of damage caused to military objectives in the Zuara area was not immediately ascertainable after this ear-splitting, dazzling attack, but obviously [it] was heavy. Great fires, brilliant explosions and a pall of heavy black smoke silhouetted for miles against a background of silvery moonlight and still clearly seen after we were again many miles at sea, bore witness to that.

All plans for this bold stroke against the forward Axis forces only a scant 20 miles away from the Tunisian border – designed to destroy military stores and installations and to hamper transport by damaging roads – were naturally kept secret.

Not until we were well at sea were we informed of the nature of our mission, which was the first of its kind in the eastern Mediterranean in many months. Announcement of the plans by the captain set officers and men alike buzzing with eagerness to get on with the job of smacking the Nazis and their stooges.

Once again, I was the only American with the fleet, and it was not at all surprising to me – after sailing on other ships in recent very successful attacks on Axis shipping – that all hands were eager to smash at enemy-held shores regardless of what unknown dangers might be lurking behind the darkened coastline.

The night was virtually perfect for bombardment. A brilliant full moon rode high in the sky and shone so bright, one could read without difficulty the labels of various gadgets of the ship's bridge. For the first time in many days, the Mediterranean – recently whipped by north-west gales – was dead calm, and sparkling in the moonlight.

Ahead of us, another cruiser (the sister ship, HMS 'Cleopatra') cut a majestic swathe in the moonlit waters and left a sparkling wake through which this sleek, speedy powerful fighting ship sped with an almost silken rustle.

Reaching a position west of Zuara, we altered course, turning broadside to the shoreline, which already was faintly visible. Soon, the outline of the Zuara lighthouse came into view and then came the order of Rear Admiral A.J. Power – First Commanding Officer of the famous HMS 'Ark Royal' – to open fire.

HMS *Euryalus* in action. An enemy aircraft dives, as shells explode all around it.

With a blinding flash and a rib-rocking roar, a score of Naval guns blasted more than a ton of high-explosive shells at this Axis target. Before our ship had time to recover from her first reactionary shudder, there came another salvo and then another and another.

In the distance the whump whump whump of exploding shells ashore could be heard. Suddenly, a brilliant sheet of red flame shot skyward from the target area and a tremendous column of inky smoke curled upward and then levelled off, hanging low as it drifted westward in the wind.

Into the fairly wide area illuminated by the fires, these warships pumped round after round of screaming shells – more than four hundred of them aggregating many, many tons – each of them seeming to leave a white crease in the sky as it hurtled toward its target.

The great billows of black smoke clearly indicated that gasoline for the Tunis-bound tanks and aircraft had been set afire, and from the volume of smoke, it appeared that a great dump was ablaze. Then came a series of explosions as other shells hit. Some of them were sharp, brilliant explosions; the type one would expect when an ammunition dump was hit. Others were dull, red blasts and still others seemed to be a cluster of sparks – as though something very solid was hit, disintegrated and tossed willy-nilly into the air.

That the Axis forces, busily engaged in the serious occupation of evacuation, never expected to be struck so far forward, almost at the Tunisian border while they were running away from forces already marching into Tripoli, was obvious. The withering shellfire from these ships brought forth not even so much as a single gun blast from a shore battery. The only firing from (the) shore was red tracer anti-aircraft fire aimed at our Star shells and clearly indicating the 'Gerries' and 'Ities' thought they were aircraft flares and that they were being attacked from the air.

Meanwhile, from their almost completely evacuated airfield in the area, the Axis managed to get one aircraft skyward, but it remained strictly non-combatant, circling us at a respectful distance and never firing a single shot.

Gunnery Office
24th July 1943

<u>H.M.S. EURYALUS – SUMMARY OF AMMUNITION FIRED AT THE ENEMY BETWEEN 16th JULY 1941 AND 18th JULY 1943</u>

5.25-inch H.E. at aircraft	6,714
5.25-inch H.E. in 5 bombardments	951
5.25-inch S.A.P. at Italian Fleet	421
5.25-inch S.A.P. in 1 bombardment	60
Total 5.25-inch shell (less Starshell):	8,146
5.25-inch Starshell in 2 bombardments and at 1 U-Boat	74
2-Pdr. H.E. Pom-Pom	8,572
Oerlikon H.E.	7,217

Thus, in 2 years, H.M.S. Euryalus has: -

Fired just over 24,000 rounds of all types at the enemy, and
Has worn out and changed 18 in number 5.25-inch gun barrels.

Signed C.K.S. Aylwin
Lieut. Comdr. (G).

HMS *Euryalus* in action. All guns point skywards in a particularly heavy engagement.